COLLE
SUGARS & CREAMERS

AN IDENTIFICATION GUIDE TO AMERICAN GLASSWARE

VOLUME TWO: FENTON - HEISEY

BY SHELLY YERGENSEN

Maple Creek Media
Hampstead ◊ Maryland ◊ United States

This book does not make any attempt to set market prices for items shown in this book. A number of factors including the item condition, the market location, the venue through which the item was sold, and the overall appeal of the design or pattern can affect the assessed value for an item. All listed measurements are approximate. Measurements have been taken either from original company catalogs or from the item itself.

All information contained in this publication is derived from the author's independent research. Neither the author nor the publisher make any warranties of any kind, expressed or implied, with regard to the material or documentation included in this book. Neither the author nor the publisher shall be liable in any event for incidental or consequential damages in connection with, or arising out of, the furnishing, performance, or use of this material.

Unless otherwise noted, all text and photographs contained in this book are from the collection of the author. This book is not sponsored, endorsed, or otherwise affiliated with any of the companies whose products are represented herein. The opinions, beliefs, and viewpoints which are presented in this publication are expressed solely by the author and do not necessarily reflect the opinions, beliefs and viewpoints of Old Line Publishing, LLC or Maple Creek Media. Old Line Publishing and Maple Creek Media are not responsible for the accuracy of any of the information contained in this publication.

ISBN-13: 9780990739227
ISBN-10: 0990739228

MAPLE CREEK MEDIA

P.O. Box 624
Hampstead, MD 21074
Toll-Free Phone: 1-877-866-8820
Toll-Free Fax: 1-877-778-3756
Email: info@maplecreekmedia.com
Website: www.maplecreekmedia.com

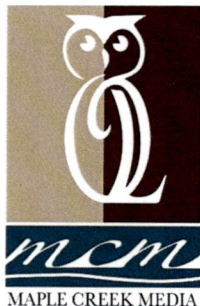

~To my husband, Brad~

My heart to you is given:
Oh, do give yours to me;
We'll lock them up together,
And throw away the key.

~ Frederick Saunders ~

ACKNOWLEDGEMENTS

I wrote in the first book in this series, *It takes a village to write a book like this*. While that's not a terribly original statement, it is so true that I have to open with this sentence again.

I've rapidly learned that my skill lies in compiling large amounts of data into a usable format, but without the research done by others before me and the knowledge that was generously shared with me, I would not have the quality or quantity of data that I present here. My ability to complete this book falls squarely on the support I received from my patient and loving husband and my good friend, and glass collecting soul-sister, Karen Plott. Thanks to modern technology, Karen and I have not let the miles that separate us keep us from sharing our love of glass and especially sugars and creamers. Her stories about me vaulting over a mahogany bureau and slapping her hand in an antique mall in Denver saying, *It's mine*, are grossly exaggerated. I'm pretty sure it was only a small footstool that I stepped over. We have spent hours on the phone, shared thousands of photos, discussed real and imaginary nuances, shipped glass across the country to one another repeatedly, and teased each other mercilessly over both of our failing memories. Seriously, thousands of photos, you have no idea.

Once again, most of the photos in this book come to you because of the generosity of others, not because I have a massive collection of rare and hard to find pieces. I am forever grateful to my other sugar and creamer collecting friends: Brandon Dowd, Dick Ladd, Jean & Vic Laermans, Dave Lippert, Glynis McCain, and Kay & Dave Tucker. Their observations and contributions have given me information I could not have gained on my own and their collections have given you a wealth of beautiful photos. In addition, Brandon Dowd offered to edit this work before I submitted it for publication; and it was his knowledge of sugars and creamers as well as good grammar that has kept me from making some of the same kinds of mistakes that tripped me up with the first book. Thank you again, Brandon. You've been a good and trusted friend.

The Fenton chapter was not possible without the input from glass authors, John Walk, Renée & Dave Shetlar, and the late Tom Smith. The Fostoria American pages would not have been as informative if not for the photos submitted by Pat & Dennis Early. Mike Sabo, president of the H.C. Fry Glass Society, contributed greatly to the Fry chapter. The Heisey chapter is where I learned to just let go and let the experts lead me where they would. John Martinez, Ted Sheets and a gentleman who prefers to remain anonymous provided me with photos, knowledge and insight into the delightful world of Heisey glass. By far and away, the person who contributed the most to my Heisey education and the thoroughness of that chapter was Dennis Headrick. I could have never duplicated his contribution even if I had spent a decade researching Heisey sugars and creamers. Dennis was so patient and so generous with his time, his photos, and his good humor. I cannot begin to thank him adequately. I hope that I did justice to all of these kind folks in respecting their contributions and representing them accurately.

The following other people contributed glass, photos, historical or personal knowledge: 9hibiscus, Inez Austin, Doug Black, Suzanne Black, Michael Bockham, Miriam Boyle, Jane Cardinal, Bob Carlson, Ckris Cord, Joyce & Jim Coverston, Vicki Curran, Nick Daemous, Lora Jo Davis, Mike Diesso, Joan Rich Dishman, Pat & Dennis Early, Dorothy Evans, Tom Felt, Lew Fisher, Lyle Fokken, Frank Forsythe, Barry Funk, Helen Gilbert, Philip Hopper, Helen & Bob Jones, Gregg Jones, Beverly Kappenman, Judy Kaufman, Michael Krumme, Louis Lopilato, Dean Lowry, Carla Maningas, Ruth MacGowan, Kathy McCarney, Tom Norskov, Bob O'Grady, Lorainne Puskarich, Kevin Roberts, Craig Schenning, Darlene Shoppart, Gerri Sorrell, Susan Spirk, Ann Stephen, Vicki Stone, Frederick L.

ACKNOWLEDGEMENTS

Schwartz, Virginia Temme, Rod Toler, Dan Tyner, Margaret & Kenn Whitmyer, Marilyn Young, and John Zastowney. I regret that I was not able to use all of the photos submitted, but unfortunately I was limited to 150 pages.

Dar Simpson, thanks for being my cheerleader. Keep it up! Some days I sure needed it.

The foundation of everything I have done with this book, the previous book, and the books I still have left to write came from and is because of Tom Felt. He has been my mentor, whether he realizes it or not. He and his partner, Bob O'Grady have given me their friendship and support; and at times I've been overwhelmed by their kindness.

I am appreciative of the Museum of America Glass in West Virginia for the use of their resources and archives as well as the Rakow Library in Corning, New York. The best online research group for this genre of glass is still located at http://www.chataboutdg.com and their image library now contains 18,500 images in 900 categories. There is a very useful database and gallery of European glass at http://www.pressglas-pavillon.de/index2.html. They call their pieces "milk & sugar" and I've identified many of my unknowns by prowling through this site. There is a large collection of glass marks identified at this site: http://glassloversglassdatabase.com/marks/ats00001.html. This is an informative site but you need to register to get the full benefit.

My own Facebook page is located at: https://www.facebook.com/pages/Collectible-Sugars-and-Creamers-Books-1-2/242484375790771. Swing by and give us a "Like".

Finally, I'm sorry it took me three years to finish this book; life kept getting in the way. Thank you, my friends, for your patience. Thanks also to everyone who kept asking my editor and myself when Book Two was going to be released; it was very flattering to have you ask. This is my gift to all of you.

TABLE OF CONTENTS

INTRODUCTION: VOLUME TWO

What this book is: This is the second book in a series of volumes which identifies collectible pressed glass sugars and creamers from the twentieth century, mostly. I stayed away from children's dishes and carnival glass, mostly. I'm pretty sure I totally stayed away from American cut glass.

Terminology: If you are an English major, or just a stickler for correct grammar, my use of the self-made abbreviation *S&C* for *sugar & creamer* will drive you insane. I use it singular and plural, and in present and past tense, interchangeably and sometimes within the same paragraph. I started incorporating the abbreviation to save space in Book One and now I just like the versatility, freedom and joie de vivre of using it. There are some folks who insist that the terminology is only correct as *creamer & sugar* instead of my preferred order, *sugar & creamer*. I chose one over the other because C&S also abbreviates *cup & saucer* and I wanted to avoid any confusion. That choice was made as I started writing Book One. I like it the way it is and I'm not going to change it for future books; so try not to let that annoy you. Also, if you object to the use of the term *creamer* instead of the term *cream*, feel free to take me off your Christmas card list.

Genre: Most of the S&C shown in this book could be classified as tableware from the Depression (1920-1945ish), Elegant (1920-1955ish), and Mid-Century (1945-1975ish) eras. In some chapters if the information was available, I stepped back and moved forward in time, leaning on the term "collectible" to guide my decisions.

Value: I've said it before and I'll say it again, pricing in a book of this type is incorrect from the moment the book is written. Don't let prices in a book rule your buying decisions, let it be your guide instead. Always look at the publication date and adjust accordingly. How do you adjust accordingly? You have to do some of your own research. If you don't like research, then buy what you like if the price seems reasonable; and enjoy your glass. Promise yourself that you will not be upset if you find out that you paid 5x what an item is really worth; but do pat yourself on the back if you find that you picked up a real bargain. That is part of the fun.

If you are selling glass, my thoughts are much the same; do your research. Prices have fallen for this genre of glass, almost unilaterally and wanting the old prices to come back isn't going to make it so. When the country went into a Recession in 2008, the price of collectible S&C fell dramatically and at the time of this writing (summer 2014), the prices generally haven't recovered.

Availability: Back when I wrote Book One, if I went out to eBay and did a search under the *glass* category for the keyword *sugar*, I would typically come up with 8,000-9,000 hits. Today, that number has increased to 17,000-18,000 hits. In just three years, there are 2x the available glass sugars on eBay to buy. Add that to other online purchasing sites as well as the large number of glass dealers that now sell online; and you've got quite a wide variety of purchasing options available while sitting on your couch with a laptop. If you factor in all of the thrift shops and antique malls across the country, the amount of *collectible* glass sugars that are currently for sale is staggering. I cannot stress to you enough the value of shopping around; unless you find something legitimately scarce or rare. A current research book can help you identify those items which are scarce to rare. Keep in mind that older books might identify an item as scarce when in fact today it might be readily available due to the advent of the internet. It makes me grimace when I see folks overpay, and I see it far too often.

Pricing: Pricing is the most difficult part of writing a book like this. I keep at it because I think most people want to have a general idea of the value of their glass. EBay is still my most valuable resource because of the ability to get historical data. I'm particularly interested in scarce to rare pieces. I enjoy it when folks buy something exciting and they send me a photo to share their new purchase. If you do this, please remember to also share what you paid for the purchase. I watch active auctions and scroll through all of eBay's sold and unsold *sugar* and *creamer* data each week. This allows me to record prices which I think are pertinent and see trends as they emerge. If a buyer grossly overpays for an item, I do not record the data. An anomaly isn't a trend, nor does it indicate a nationwide price. My prices include postage as part of the total realized value. This is confusing for the lowest priced items because some items are priced lower than the cost of shipping them across the country. Use your best judgment, but anything that common might be more easily and cheaply found in your local antique mall. Modern reissues of some items may be mentioned without being priced.

As in Book 1, creamers and sugars without lids are almost always priced the same.
Creamers are typically harder to find than lid-less sugars, but prices rarely reflect that.

Organization: Chapters are organized by manufacturing company alphabetically, with individual lines being listed in an approximate date order from oldest to newest, where dates are available. I juggled this organization a bit because glass companies frequently did not cooperate with my desire to organize their wares into this fashion. Also some juggling was done so the information fit the space available on the page. I occasionally moved items out of their date sequence because I felt like they should be presented alongside another set which had a confusable resemblance.

Dates: In many cases I could only provide an approximate date.

Photos: All of the photos in this book were taken by amateur photographers, myself included. Some photographers were more skilled and some had newer equipment than others. People shared with me what they could and I am grateful for each and every contribution. I enjoy the scrapbook feel of sharing a quilt of photos and catalog reprints. I am sorry I could not include all of the photos which I collected.

Looking Ahead: This book was initially supposed to contain Fenton-Imperial chapters. But once I realized what a treasure trove of Heisey information I had, it felt criminal to cut short the Heisey chapter. That left me with the choice of being disrespectful to the Imperial chapter by making it fit into the pages that were left; or move Imperial into Book Three. I chose to respect the glass. There are just too many really great things coming up in the Imperial chapter to scrimp. The upside was I got to add some things to the Fenton, Fostoria, Fry and Hazel-Atlas chapters; which I had previously decided to leave out. You also get an appendix of tid-bits which became available after Book One was published. There isn't a downside as far as I can see. Book Three looks like it might be Imperial–Morgantown. But I never know until I layout the pages.

If you have thoughts or comments about anything in this book, please feel free to write to me or email me at shelly.yergensen@q.com. At this time I also have a Facebook page under the title of: Collectible Sugars and Creamers. Future technologies will probably bring us a more interactive social media to share our love of S&C and I look forward to that. There is still lots of information out there that can be added to this book of knowledge.

Much of Fenton's early 20th-century reputation was earned with it's beautiful Carnival glass and decorated water sets. In the 1920s, the company joined the other Elegant glass houses producing colored dinnerware lines. However, setting the table with expansive and bloated tableware lines, which had a piece of glass for every imaginable purpose, was never the company's passion. Fenton stayed in business longer than most glass companies because they were able to better determine and cater to the changes in the glass market. They kept their glass both desirable and collectible.

Crystal sugars and creamers are not typically associated with Fenton, yet in their book, *Fenton Art Glass 1907-1939, Identification & Value Guide, Second Edition*, Margaret and Kenn Whitmeyer indicate that at least thirteen different sugar and creamer sets were made in crystal and decorated in Fenton's cutting shop. The exact identity of these crystal sets are a mystery at this time.

Luckily collectors have identified a few crystal sets which were also made in Fenton's unique colors. These sets may well be part of the thirteen. And, if other colored sets appear, researchers might be able to attribute more crystal sets to Fenton.

The hexagonal set shown above is known to be Fenton because it has been found in both Cameo Opalescent and blue Stretch Glass. However, it's line number is unknown. Currently, most collectors don't realize that it is Fenton and it gets lost in the $5-$10 glut of crystal glass available in today's market.

Another early Fenton crystal set has been identified due to it also being made in the opaque glass which Fenton called Persian Blue. A rare colored catalog reprint from the mid-1910s shows the blue set and identifies it as **No. 596.** Certain line numbers were only assigned to Persian Blue items, so it is not believed to be the line number for the crystal set.

This blank is one of the ubiquitous lookalike shapes in S&C collecting which causes confusion regarding their manufacturing origin. The sugar is 2-3/8" high and 3-5/16" across. There is a large 16 pt. star in the base. The creamer is 3-3/8" high and 3-7/16" across. There is a smaller 16 pt. star in it's base. Crystal pieces have haphazardly ground bases. My blue sugar also has a ground bottom but my blue creamer does not. Be aware that during this time of hand-shaped glass, some measurements may not be exactly the same.

Time has not been kind to the white enamel flowers which were painted on No. 596 and most flowers are found today in poor condition. Note the unusual creamer above which has a lighter blue body blending out of the darker blue base.

There are at least three known lookalikes which have the same reeded handles and only slight variations in dimension. Shown below and at right is the Fenton set alongside two of these lookalikes.

Note the different bases of these lookalike sugars. Both the green and the stained yellow sugars have bases where the vertical and horizontal planes meet at a nearly perpendicular angle. But with the Fenton blue sugar, the sides curve into the bottom making a rounded base.

Shown below and directly at right are examples of another little known Fenton blank where the crystal set was identified because of the sets which were found in Fenton colors. These fine optic S&C are very difficult to find, even in crystal. There are lookalikes to this set but this Fenton sugar is unique in that the rim of the sugar climbs up each handle in an inverted V-shape. Pieces have so far been found in crystal and the colors shown here. Currently there is no known name or line number. The Stretch Glass pieces are too rare to price and only a few examples are known to exist.

Shown above are two colored creamers alongside a Fenton crystal creamer. All three pieces are similar in height, capacity and diameter. Also, all three sets have a reeded handle, which is similar in shape. The green set has no star in the base. There is a 16 pt. star in the base of the yellow stained creamer but the yellow stained sugar has an 18 pt. star in it's base. Both the Fenton sugar and creamer have 16 pt. stars. The yellow stained set has a thinner layer of glass in it's base, and it's weight is noticeably less than either the Fenton or green set. I have not been able to confirm if either of these lookalikes came in plain crystal, but my guess is that both sets can be found in crystal.

Topaz (Vaseline) creamer (no treatment) next to sugar with Stretch Glass treatment.

No known name or line number in blue stretch glass. Courtesy Renée & Dave Shetlar.

The early (circa 1910s) lines of Honeycomb & Clover and Waterlily & Cattails are known by their rather large size. Sugar containers from the early part of the 20th century were frequently large owing to sugar being served in chunks, cubes and loaves rather than granulated as it is now.

Honeycomb & Clover (left), Waterlily and Cattails (right). Honeycomb & Clover spooner with creamer (below).

Sugars with lids in either of these lines are rare. Creamers are frequently found mated with a spooner as a set. This pairing is found so often that it's likely the set was sold that way by Fenton, and the lidded sugar was taken out of production early.

Honeycomb & Clover is available in crystal, blue, and green. Green sets can be found decorated in gold. Waterlily & Cattails is available in crystal, satinized crystal, blue, green, amethyst and opaque chocolate glass. In both lines Opalescent colors are heavily preferred over plain colors with collectors.

Another early Fenton set which was available in Persian Blue also came in crystal with the same fine internal optic as shown on the previous page.

No. 599 Banded Laurel (above) and No. 580 (below). Known as No. 250 when sold in plain crystal. Catalog illustrations this column courtesy Margaret & Kenn Whitmyer.

	Creamer or Spooner	Sugar w/lid
Honeycomb & Clover, any color, plain	$15-$18	trtp
Honeycomb & Clover, any color, opalescent	$20-$25	trtp
Waterlily & Cattails, crystal, satin, blue, green	$7-$10	trtp
Waterlily & Cattails, crystal, blue, green, oplscnt	$10-$15	trtp
Waterlily & Cattails, amethyst, opalescent	$80	trtp
Waterlily & Cattails, chocolate	trtp	trtp
No. 250, plain crystal	$12	$28
No. 580, red banded crystal	trtp	trtp
No. 599, Banded Laurel	trtp	trtp

	Creamer or Sugar
No. 596, Persian Blue	$15 *
Any early crystal, with/without simple cuttings	$8-$10
Topaz or blue Stretch Glass	trtp

* Price is for pieces with "good" condition white flowers.

Stretch Glass pieces were sprayed with a metallic salt mixture after removal from the mold to give the glass an iridescent sheen. Then the glass was reheated. After reheating, an additional working of the hot pieces produced an onionskin texture. If there were non-iridized handles, they were applied after the piece cooled. Since S&C were not worked overly much, the onionskin effect is subtle. Stretch Glass differs from Carnival Glass in that Carnival Glass is worked before the metallic salts are applied.

sold for $175.00 on E-BAY JAN. 2015

No. 2, Persian Pearl Stretch Glass with cobalt handles.
Courtesy Renée & Dave Shetlar.

An hourglass shaped S&C was made by at least five different glass companies. Fenton called their version: **No. 2**. If you find a set with one of the unique Fenton treatments or colors, No. 2 is easy to identify. It is not known if the company made this shape in plain crystal but if they did, a crystal piece might be difficult to prove as Fenton due to the similarities of some of the lookalikes. Beginning In the 1920s, No. 2 was made in Stretch Glass.

No. 2, Florentine Green Stretch Glass with cobalt handles.
Courtesy Renée & Dave Shetlar.

The following Stretch Glass colors were produced: Celeste Blue, Florentine Green, Grecian Gold (crystal with marigold iridescence), Persian Pearl (crystal with white iridescence), Topaz (vaseline), and Tangerine. All of these colors came with cobalt handles except for Tangerine which came with plain tangerine colored handles. These sets range from difficult to nearly impossible to locate and are highly desirable to several groups of collectors.

Also in the 1920s, Fenton began producing No. 2 in the distinctive **Rib Optic** pattern. The green opalescent set was sold at least through 1926; while the blue opalescent set was known to be sold into the late 1930s. This might explain why blue is easier to locate. Note the low attachment position of the top of the creamer handle. This is unique. Should you find a crystal creamer with a dropped handle like this, it is probably Fenton.

No. 2, Rib Optic.
Green Opalescent creamer, Blue Opalescent sugar.

No. 2, Rib Optic in Cameo Opalescent,
probably made in the 1920s.

No. 3, Stretch Glass in Persian Pearl and Aquamarine.
Courtesy Brandon Dowd.

The sugar and creamer shape known as **No. 3** was sold in both Stretch and transparent colors during the 1920s. No. 3 pieces were press-molded, and the handles are the same color as the rest of the piece. I have seen No. 3 in black, cobalt, Jade, aqua, pink, and Cameo Opalescent. Stretch glass colors known are: Persian Pearl, Aquamarine, Velva Rose, Tangerine, Florentine Green and Grecian Gold.

No 3 in black. Black Diamond Optic dinnerware pieces were made, but every black S&C which I have been able to examine does not have the diamond optic pattern inside. Courtesy Beverly Kappenman.

No. 1502, Orchid Diamond Optic with painted flowers on base. Courtesy Jean & Vic Laermans.

Unusual No. 1502, Diamond Optic in Celeste Blue Stretch Glass. Also known in Velva Rose. Courtesy Renée & Dave Shetlar.

In the late 1920s, Fenton modified the No. 3 blank by adding an optic pattern inside the pieces. The resulting sugar and creamer was included in their **No. 1502, Diamond Optic** dinnerware line.

Diamond Optic remained in the Fenton catalogs into the mid-1930s. The set was originally available only in green, pink and Orchid. Soon afterward the S&C were also made in Tangerine, cobalt, red and aqua. Note that red pieces can be anywhere between a deep, pure ruby to red with obvious yellow highlights (amberina).

Sugar or Creamer	#3	#3 (stretch)	#1502
Crystal (Pearl)		$25	
Pink (Velva Rose)	$13	$25	$12**
Green (Florentine Gr)		$35	$12
Aqua (Aquamarine)	$16	$22	$14
Celeste Blue		$45	**
Tangerine		$60	$45
Red			$14 *
Orchid			$36
Black	$23		
Jade	$17		
Cobalt	$27		$32
Vaseline (Topaz)	$37		
Grecian Gold	$16		
Cameo Opalescent		$30	

* Solid red with no trace of amberina add 50%
** No. 1502 pieces in Stretch Glass are trtp.

Sugar or Creamer	#2	#2 (stretch)
Green Opalescent Rib Optic	$70	
Blue Opalescent Rib Optic	$45	
Cameo Opalescent Rib Optic	trtp	
All colors		trtp

There is no catalog proof that Fenton sold the Diamond Optic S&C on the 9" tray but if a tray can be acquired, S&C collectors like to display the pieces together.

There is no known name or line number for the set shown above. I call this sugar and creamer **Stella** for identification purposes. Stella is also known in French Opalescent Rib Optic and French Opalescent Coin Dot. French Opalescent is Fenton's name for crystal glass with a white opalescent treatment and examples are shown later in this chapter. Stella is too rare to price.

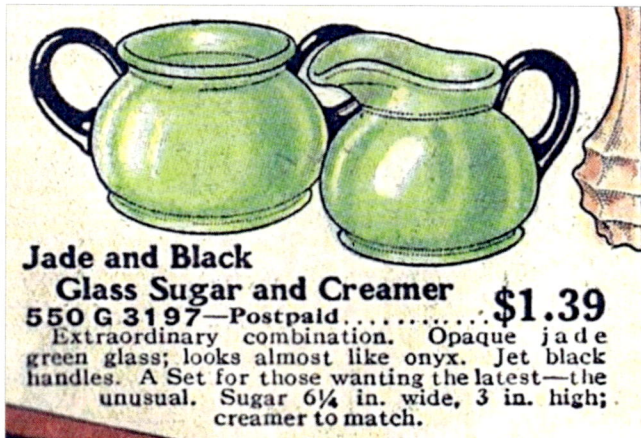

Jade and Black
Glass Sugar and Creamer
550 G 3197—Postpaid..........$1.39
Extraordinary combination. Opaque jade green glass; looks almost like onyx. Jet black handles. A Set for those wanting the latest—the unusual. Sugar 6¼ in. wide, 3 in. high; creamer to match.

1930 Montgomery Ward catalog.

Sugar and Creamer
Cleverly modeled of black glassware, which has come into fashionable favor. With your crystal this Set makes a stunning effect. Simple yet so impressive! Cap. 6 oz.
550 G 3157— Postpaid...**59¢**

1930 Montgomery Ward catalog.

No. 1611, Georgian, was originally introduced in a 1930 brochure as *Agua Caliente*. It appears that the name change to Georgian happened almost immediately. I like the name Agua Caliente. It was a casino and hotel in Tijuana, Mexico from 1928-1935. In 1932 my grandparents met in Los Angeles, fell in love, and snuck over the border to the Agua Caliente resort to elope. True story!

Available in crystal, amber, lt. green, pink, red, cobalt, black and Jade. Red is the easiest to locate while crystal and pastel colors are the most difficult.

No. 1611, Agua Caliente from a 1930s Fenton brochure.

No. 100, Wide Rib, with it's concentric rings was made in lt. green, pink, black, cobalt and Jade. Black is the easiest to locate and cobalt is the most difficult. The set was probably also made in crystal but I cannot confirm that. If it were, that would make crystal the most difficult to locate.

No. 100, Wide Rib. Courtesy Glynis McCain.

No. 1700, flat Lincoln Inn. Courtesy Kay & Dave Tucker.

No. 1700, footed Lincoln Inn in light green opalescent. Courtesy Jean & Vic Laermans.

No. 1700, Lincoln Inn was one of Fenton's dinnerware lines during the Depression era. Lincoln Inn remained in the catalogs from the late 1920s to the late 1930s. The Lincoln Inn S&C came in a flat and a footed variety. The flat sets are the most difficult to find. The flat S&C appeared in the 1928 catalog and the footed sets appeared in the 1929 trade journals. To date I have only seen flat sets in crystal, light blue and medium green. The flat set was reissued in crystal in 1940 through a specialty gift catalog.

Red Lincoln Inn sugars and creamers seem to purposely have a yellow foot as they all appear that way. Black sets are reported to exist, but I have not had the opportunity of seeing black, so I can't verify that color. Jade and opalescent green sets are the most difficult to find.

The **No. 349** crystal S&C were sold with the Wisteria satin-etching from 1937–1938. No. 349 was a Fenton line number and not just the number for this S&C. While Fenton did several different satin-etchings similar to Wisteria, this is the only pattern I have seen on the S&C. This set is difficult to find. Fenton produced a small bowl similar to the No. 349 sugar in several colors. The bowl has a more flared edge and it's frequently misrepresented as a sugar, but it is not.

No. 349 with Wisteria etching. Courtesy Karen Plott.

Sugar or Creamer	#1700	#100 Wide Rib	#1611 Georgian
Crystal	$14		$12
Amber			$8
Lt. green, pink	$38	$15	$28
Aqua	$45		trtp
Lt. blue, med. green	$50		
Red	$30		$13
Cobalt	$25	$28	$18
Opalescent green	$70		
Black		$16	$25
Jade	trtp	$24	$30

	Sugar or Creamer
No. 349 Wisteria etching	$40

No. 1639, Elizabeth, was part of a small dinnerware line in the early 1930s. S&C collectors love this pattern because most of the pieces are bi-colored. Some colors have a scalloped footprint while others have a nearly square footprint..

No. 1639 scalloped footprint vs. square footprint.

Note the circa 1930 catalog reprint below which shows a short creamer. In comparison, the photo of an actual blue set directly below that shows a tall creamer. I have never seen a short creamer in any color. Perhaps Fenton introduced the set originally with a short creamer and then changed their mind after a short run of the set. I would love to hear if anyone has seen a short creamer in any color.

1639 Sugar   1639 Creamer

No. 1639, Elizabeth with scalloped foot. Courtesy Jean & Vic Laermans.

The scarcity of Elizabeth makes it difficult to discern exactly which colors the S&C were made in. Other tableware pieces in the Elizabeth line came in the following color combinations: cobalt with black foot, red with cobalt foot, and lilac with Moonstone (pearl) foot. These colors are possible in the sugar and creamer, but I have not been able to verify if the set was actually made in any of these combinations.

No. 1639, Elizabeth with scalloped foot. Courtesy Brandon Dowd.

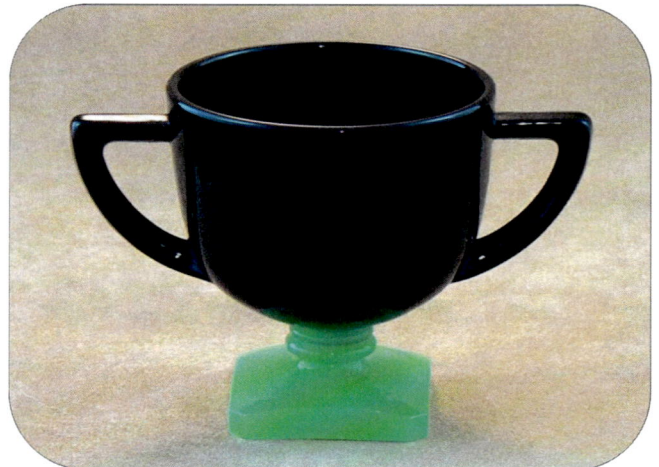

No. 1639, Elizabeth with square foot.

#1639 Elizabeth	Sugar or Creamer
Royal blue with crystal foot	$48
Red with crystal foot	$40
Red with red foot	$55
Black with Jade foot	$75
Jade with black foot	trtp
Jade with Moonstone foot	trtp
Jade with Jade foot	trtp

In the late 1930s, the **No. 1900, Cape Cod Crystal,** S&C were introduced. They appear to have been part of a small dinnerware line with additional gift items. In the 1950s when Fenton reissued this S&C in milk glass, they changed the official name to **No. 1903, Daisy & Button.** The S&C are known for their little wing-shaped handles. Cape Cod Crystal did not have a crimped rim and the colors I have seen are amber, Aquamarine, Cape Cod Green, Cape Cod Blue, and vaseline. A 1937 brochure indicated that No. 1900 tableware items came in other colors, so the sugar and creamer may have been made in other colors as well.

No. 1900, Cape Cod Crystal in Vaseline (above) and Aquamarine (below). Courtesy Karen Plott.

In the late 1930s or early 1940s, a French and Blue Opalescent sugar and creamer with crimped rims was released. The Opalescent sets were also known as No. 1900 but don't appear to be part of the Cape Cod Crystal line.

Note the different levels of opalescence in the crystal set shown. S&C collectors find it most desirable if their sets match each other in the level of opalescence. The more opalescence a piece has, the more desirable it is to collectors, particularly those who specialize in Fenton.

Note the two similar green sets shown below. The set on the left is Spruce Green, a recent Fenton color. The set on the right is the original Cape Cod Green (aka Stiegel Green). The 1930s pieces were worked into a shorter, more rounded profile.

Spruce Green (left) and Cape Cod Green (right) color comparison. Courtesy Karen Plott.

Blue and French (crystal) Opalescent.

#1900 or Cape Cod Crystal	Sugar or Creamer
Crystal, amber	$6
Cape Cod Green	$9
Vaseline, aqua	$11
Cape Cod Blue (royal blue)	$22
French Opalescent, crimped rim	$11
Blue Opalescent, crimped rim	$15

No. 389
Individual Sugar and Cream Set

No. 389
Oil

No. 389
Mustard & Spoon

No. 389
Sugar and Cream Set

Fenton began selling **Hobnail** lines in the 1930s but it was the opalescent Hobnail of the 1940s that established it's popularity. The first Hobnail sugars and creamers were the **No. 389** sets. Both the *tall-389* and the *squat-389* had the same number in the catalogs.

While the vast majority of these pieces are opalescent, once in a while relatively unpopular non-opalescent sets surface. What folks may not realize is that the non-opalescent sets are thought to have been produced in the late 1930s, before the opalescent colors. Knowing that these pieces are older may help increase their collectability one day.

Non-Opalescent blue (above) and green (below) No. 389 tall and squat. Both photos courtesy John Walk.

Green Opalescent tall-389 (above) and Cranberry Opalescent tall-389 (below). Both photos courtesy Kay & Dave Tucker.

The yellowish-green shade which was eventually used for the Green Opalescent color run was introduced in 1940 and then discontinued in 1941. This is probably due to the USA's entrance into WWII. The chemicals needed to make this shade may have became scarce or completely unavailable.

The tall-389 set was made in plain green, plain blue, French (crystal), Green, Topaz, Blue, and Cranberry Opalescent. Note that the green set shown has green molded handles while the cranberry set has crystal handles which were applied by hand. This makes the Cranberry set more desirable.

In 1944, a small, special-order of Wisteria Opalescent (lavender) Hobnail items were made exclusively for Sherwin-Williams Paints. This very brief run included the tall-389 S&C. These Wisteria sets are too rare to price.

Topaz Opalescence was introduced in 1941. Both the Cranberry and Topaz Opalescent tall-389 were discontinued in 1944. The squat-389 was never made in Cranberry, but it was made in Topaz from 1941-1944. The tall Topaz Opalescent set was reissued in the 1980s for a secondary market. Newer pieces will have a Fenton logo.

The squat-389 set was made in plain green, plain blue, Topaz, Blue, and French Opalescent. None of the squat sets have achieved the beloved status and prices of the tall sets. Both Blue and French Opalescent were produced for 15+ years, being discontinued in the late 1950s.

Different levels of opalescence are common from piece to piece. You may spend some time looking for a similar level of opalescence in both pieces. While matching your blue pieces, note that you may find different shades of blue.

Sometime after the 1950 catalog, Fenton redid their line numbering system. The squat set was renamed **No. 3900**, and the tall-389 was renamed **No. 3901**.

For a short window in 1943, the tall-389 set was produced in Rose Overlay. Rose Overlay is pink glass cased over opal glass. The Rose Overlay set had the same crystal applied handles as the Cranberry set. Applied handles were an extra step in the process which made these pieces more expensive to produce. It also makes these pieces more desirable to today's collector. Rose Overlay is trtp.

Rose Overlay Hobnail. Courtesy John Walk.

Both of the No. 389 sets appeared in white milk glass in the Fenton catalogs from the 1950s into the 1970s. 1950 is generally accepted as the date when Fenton began producing these two sets in milk glass. It's interesting that the 1940 catalog shown above indicates that the tall-389 set was being made in "milk colors". I have no information as to what these milk colors might be, or if this is a reference to the use of opalescence.

The No. 389 7-pc condiment set, which sat on a round center-handle tray, was introduced in 1950. It consisted of the squat sugar and creamer, the 389 oil, the 389 flat shakers, and the 389 mustard with spoon and lid. This set came in French Opalescent, Blue Opalescent and milk glass. When Fenton renumbered its Hobnail pieces, the 7-pc condiment set became known as **No. 3809**. Notice the different tray bottoms shown below. The tray directly below (left) is a pedestal design which must have been quickly replaced as it only appears in the 1950 catalog. The bowl-style tray is more commonly seen, and it is shown in the catalogs from the early 1950s through the late 1960s. Both trays appear to be the same, just turned upside down from one another. There are also two different handles shown and the handle on the pedestal tray looks to be a replacement. The simple handle directly below (right) is older. For a brief time in the 1970s, No. 3809 was re-released in milk glass.

No. 3809 7-pc condiment set with pedestal base. Courtesy Helen Gilbert.

No. 3809 7-pc condiment set with bowl base. Note the different shade of blue on the cruet indicating it might not have been original to this set. Photo courtesy Jane Cardinal.

No. 3809 7-pc condiment set with bowl base. Courtesy Brandon Dowd.

#389 Sugar or Creamer	Tall (#3901)	Squat (#3900)
Milk glass	<$5	<$5
Green, no opal	$14	$6
Blue, no opal	$12	$8
French Opalescent	$8	$5
Blue Opalescent	$9	$7
Topaz Opalescent	$18	$15
Green Opalescent	$23	
Cranberry Opalescent	$52	

	White	French	Blue
Condiment tray, bowl-type	$18	$48	$75

In the 1948 catalog, the **No. 680, Silver Crest**, S&C had ruffled rims and an actual applied crest of crystal. The sugar had no handles, and the creamer had a reeded crystal applied handle. This design was in the Fenton catalog for only one year, and in 1949 the set was redesigned to the more well known, non-crested bulb shape with it's crimped crystal handle.

During the 18 years it was in production, Silver Crest remained virtually unchanged. Virtually unchanged doesn't mean that there aren't slight differences which can be found. Older catalog pages show a noticeably shorter profile to the sugar with a pronounced flare to the rim. Newer sugars are taller and less flared. Overall, the shorter and squattier the pieces are, the more desirable they seem to be to collectors.

Rare Silver Crest S&C are found with the painted decoration *Violets in the Snow* which Fenton sold in the late 1960s. This decoration is generally thought to have not been painted on the Silver Crest sugar and creamer; but sets are out there.

Silver Crest 1948 catalog (above) and 1949 catalog (below).

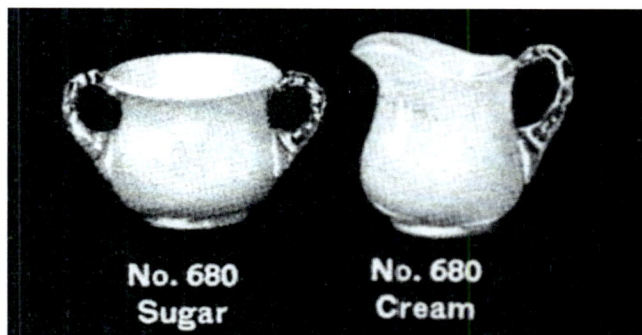
No. 680 Sugar   No. 680 Cream

Violets in the Snow sample (right).

Scarce dark green uncrimped handle (left) next to the more common Emerald, crimped handle (right). Courtesy Jean & Vic Laermans.

The set shown above was not decorated by Fenton Art Glass or any of it's artists. This set was hand painted by the independent artist, Vicki Curren. It is dated 2014 and numbered as one of a kind. The Crest pieces are an excellent canvas for art such as this and time will tell if Fenton collectors gravitate toward pieces like this for their collections. Photo and information courtesy Vicki Curren.

The painted decoration above is known as Charleton Pegged Rose by Ables, Wasserberg & Co. This company was known for painted decorations on Fenton Crest pieces. The pieces are marked only with a stamp that says "hand painted". Courtesy Ann Stephen.

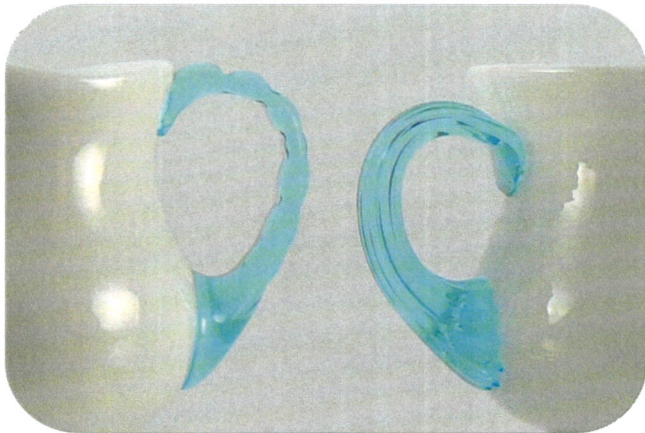

*Normal crimped handle (left) next to unusual reeded handle (right).
Photos above and below courtesy Jean & Vic Laermans.*

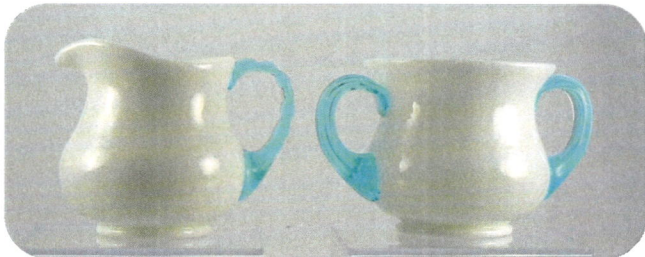

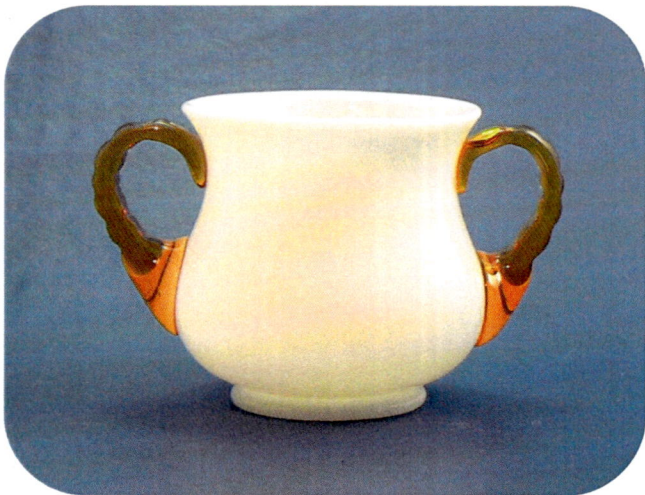

Gold Crest sugars appear on rare occasions. They were probably produced in or around 1963 when Fenton did most of their other Gold Crest items. So far, all I've seen are sugars but I'm told two Gold Crest creamers are known to exist.

The **No. 33, Coin Dot**, creamer and sugar is a Fenton set that most S&C collectors want to own. Even collectors who aren't big Fenton fans seek out this set. The creamer is flat, with a crystal crimped handle, and the sugar looks like a pencil cup. This simple design was in the Fenton catalogs for only a couple of years in the late 1940s.

You will sometimes find the No. 33 sugar incorrectly married to the **No. 1924** 4" cream pitcher. The No. 1924 cream pitcher is taller and narrower than No. 33. No. 1924 did not have a matching sugar.

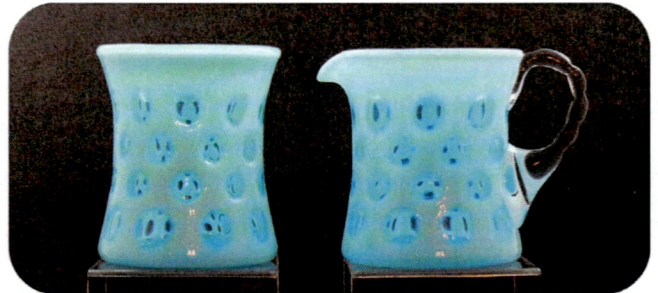

No. 33, Coin Dot in Blue Opalescent (above) and Cranberry Opalescent (below). Both photos courtesy Kay & Dave Tucker.

#680 Crests	Sugar or Creamer
Silver Crest (1948)	$36 sugar / $52 creamer
Silver Crest (1949 forward)	$18 *
Emerald Crest	$33 ** / $36 dark green handles
Aqua Crest	$46
Gold Crest	trtp

* Silver Crest with Violets-In-the-Snow decoration trtp.
** Pegged Rose decoration price 3x plain Emerald Crest.

#33 Coin Dot	French	Blue	Cranberry
Opalescent sugar	$22	$30	$50
Opalescent creamer	$28	$39	$68

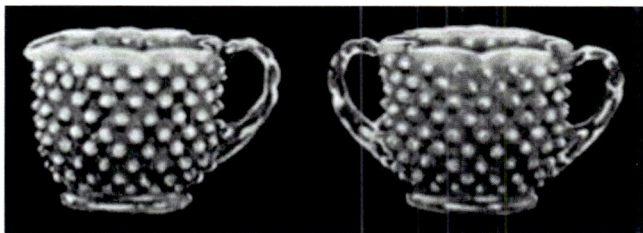

The 1949 catalog calls the star-crimped hobnail S&C (above) both **Nos. 3** and **389**. By the time this set was being produced in milk glass, the catalog line number had changed to **No. 3906**. To avoid confusion with other Fenton items, I refer to this set with the 1950s designation of No. 3906.

The earliest versions of No. 3906 had a hand applied crystal handle. This handle style was still being sold in the 1953 catalog. Sometime after that, the sugar and creamer were changed to a mold handle. These later pieces had a handle which was the same color as the bowl, and the opalescent treatment extended down the handles. The applied crystal handle is significantly more difficult to find and more expensive for collectors to purchase.

Close-up of applied crystal handle next to mold handle.
Courtesy Jean & Vic Laermans.

As late as 2010, Fenton has reissued No. 3906 in French Opalescent and a slightly different shade of opalescent blue which they called Robins Egg Blue. Both of these reissues will have the Fenton logo, so check for that if you want to make sure you are purchasing vintage stock.

Fenton produced an unusual No. 3906 with a non-crimped rim. This set was probably produced between 1953 and 1956 (because of the mold handle and because opalescent hobnail was discontinued in 1956.) These sets are scarce but their prices are very reasonable.

No. 3906 with non-ruffled rim. Courtesy Brandon Dowd.

The early S&C sets with the applied handles came in Blue, French and Cranberry Opalescent. The later versions with the mold handles came in Blue and French Opalescent.

Cranberry sets only came with the applied handle. This was largely due to the process required to create the Opalescent Cranberry. It is a heat sensitive color which is made from casing the cranberry glass with French Opalescent glass. After the pieces were formed, they were reheated and the areas that got the hottest turned white. The variability of this process resulted in limited production and wide fluctuations in appearance. The complex cased-glass process made a mold handle impossible.

Cranberry Opalescent pieces are scarce and a well-matched set is typically made from buying both pieces as orphans and bringing the two together in a private marriage ceremony.

Blue Opalescent No. 3906. Courtesy Kay & Dave Tucker.

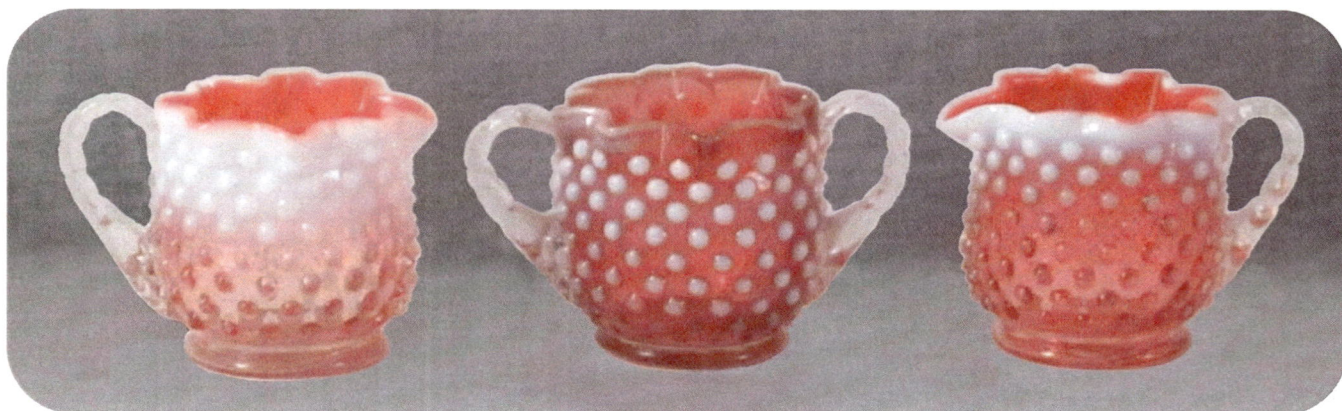

Different levels of reheating produced different levels of opalescence. Above are samples of the wide variations which can be found on Cranberry Opalescent sugars and creamers. Courtesy Kevin Roberts.

Beginning in the early 1950s, No. 3906 Hobnail was produced in white and colored milk glass. White production began in 1950 and lasted for 30+ years. The pastel colors of pink, blue, green and turquoise lasted for a short time in the mid-1950s.

The earliest milk glass sets can be identified by the relative thinness .of the glass and a slight translucence. This effect can be seen the easiest with the Rose pastel pieces. The early milk glass formula ultimately proved to break too easily and it was eventually replaced with the thicker, opaque milk glass which became a Fenton mainstay.

No. 3906 was made in transparent Colonial Amber and Colonial Pink in the 1960s. From 1976-1979, No. 3906 was made in the heat sensitive opaque color that Fenton called **Rosalene.** The best Rosalene shading should go from light to dark pink.

Rosalene. Courtesy Jean & Vic Laermans.

From left to right, Blue, Aqua and Green Pastel milk glass (above) and Rose Pastel milk glass (below).

No. 3917 3-pc. set consisting of the No. 3906 sugar and creamer and the No. 3879 2-place tray. Courtesy Brandon Dowd.

As of 2011, No. 3906 in white milk glass has been reproduced in China and is being sold through the *Miles Kimball* mail-order catalog. I got a kick out of learning that *Hobnail* was written as *Hoenail* on the sugar packaging and *Hondail* on the creamer packaging.

Original (left) reproduction (right). Notice the elongated handle shape on the Chinese reproduction giving it a wider footprint looking down from the top.

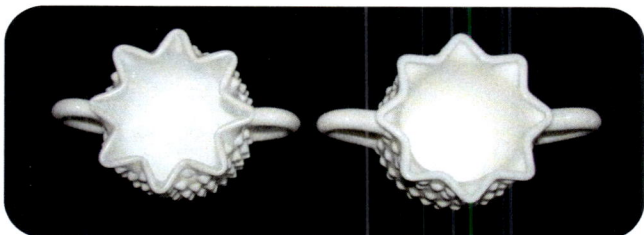

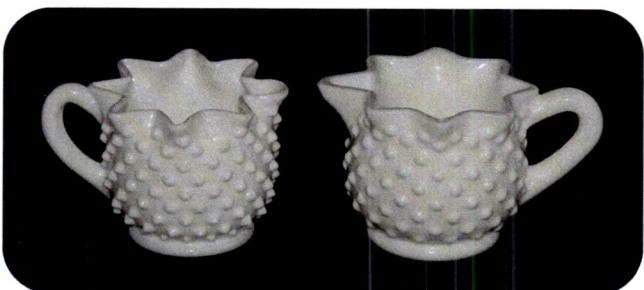

Original (left) reproduction (right). Notice the carefully pointed creamer spout on the Chinese version. Also notice how much thicker the Chinese glass is. All photos courtesy Tom Norskov.

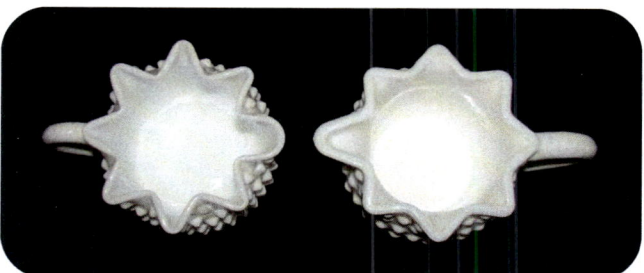

The following information was provided by Tom Norskov: The reproduction S&C are much heavier than the Fenton pieces. The Fenton creamer weighs 9.0 ounces and the reproduction weighs 15.5 ounces. The Fenton sugar weighs 9.5 ounces and the reproduction weighs 15.2 ounces. To the top of the creamer and sugar bodies, the Fenton creamer is 2-7/8" tall versus 2-15/16" for the reproduction. The Fenton sugar is 2-13/16" tall and the Chinese sugar is 3" tall. Both makers measurements may vary from piece to piece.

The hobs are rounded on the Chinese pieces while Fenton hobs are pointed. When looking straight down on each piece you will notice the Fenton pieces are star-shaped while the Chinese ones are more squared and symmetrical. There is no makers mark on the Chinese pieces only a foil sticker saying *Made in China*.

#3906 Hobnail	Sugar or Creamer
Milk glass	$6 with logo / $10 without
Pastel green, turquoise milk	$17
Pastel pink, blue milk	$19
Rosalene	$27
Amber transparent	$10
Pink transparent	$19
French Opal, no crimp rim, mold handle	$8
French Opal, mold handle	$12 **
French Opal, applied handle	$18
Blue Opal, mold handle	$13
Blue Opal, applied handle	$38
Cranberry Opal, applied handle	$80
#3879 2-place tray, milk glass	$14
#3879 2-place tray, French Opal	$34
#3879 2-place tray, Blue Opal	$65

** Reissued. Look for pieces without Fenton logo

Fenton white milk glass S&C made after 1974 will have the Fenton mark, but the company made No. 3906 for 20+ years before they began marking their pieces, so there are a lot of unmarked sets out there.

No. 1890, Priscilla. Courtesy Kay & Dave Tucker.

No. 1890, Priscilla, was introduced in 1950 along with a small number of matching tableware items. The line apparently had less than stellar popularity with buyers as it was discontinued in the middle of 1952. It's interesting to note that pieces appear with their stickers intact on a regular basis. In 1966, some Priscilla items were made for and sold by LG Wright. The S&C were not among those items. Colors include crystal, green and aqua.

No. 1890, Priscilla. Courtesy Jean & Vic Laermans.

Possible one-of-a-kind Lime Opalescent Spiral Optic creamer in the New World shape. Courtesy John Walk.

New World, No. 7304 in Dusk. Courtesy John Walk.

In 1953, Fenton introduced the **New World** line. Cataloged as **No. 7304**, the black S&C with its gray interior (known as Dusk) was apparently the least appreciated out of all the New World S&C. The Dusk set was discontinued after less than a year.

The vertically striped S&C sets in the New World line were called **No. 1604, Rib Optic**. The Lime Opalescent Rib Optic was discontinued by 1954, and even the beloved cranberry color only lasted until 1955. Some of the Cranberry pieces are found with a slightly ruffled rim. Collectors seem to prefer the straight rim pieces giving them a 20% price edge.

New World, Cranberry Rib Optic. Courtesy Lew Fisher.

#1890 Priscilla	Crystal	Green	Blue
Sugar or creamer	$6	$8	$12

New World	Dusk	Lime Opal	Cranberry Opal
Sugar	trtp	$65	$80
Creamer	trtp	$80	$95

Cranberry Polka Dot, 1955 catalog.

In 1955, the Cranberry **Polka Dot** line was introduced to consumers. Polka Dot is a small French Opalescent dot on a cranberry field. The **No. 2204** set consisted of the **No. 2293** sugar-shaker and the **No. 2261** creamer. The sugar-shaker has a metal lid.

In 1956, the same blanks were made in a new color known as Polka Dot in Ruby Overlay. The **No. 2461** creamer and **No. 2493** sugar-shaker were never sold as a set but collectors put them together just like the Cranberry Polka Dot set. Ruby Overlay is red glass with crystal cased on the outside. The polka dot like indentations are in the crystal layer. The sugar-shaker was in catalogs for 1 year, while the creamer lasted for 12 years, so you get an idea of how difficult it is to put this set together.

Collectors who specialize in sugar-shakers typically snag any No. 2493 which comes up for auction. In 1958, the No. 2461 creamer was sold in Jamestown Blue Polka Dot but no sugar-shaker was released to be its partner.

2461 RO
Creamer

Polka Dot	Cranberry	Ruby Overlay
Sugar-shaker w/metal lid	$76	$55
Creamer	$38	$27

The **No. 7006, Swirl,** sugar and creamer was introduced in 1954, and discontinued in late 1955 or early 1956. This appears to be the first sugar with a glass lid that Fenton produced. The stubby finial looks like it was difficult to hold onto and not many of the lids have survived. This is one of the few lines that came in the pastel milk glass colors of pink, green and blue as well as white. From a photo you might think that these pieces are chunky and heavy but they aren't, they are surprisingly delicate.

No. 7006, Swirl in Green Pastel Courtesy Brandon Dowd.

In 1958 Fenton introduced the **No. 6601, Rib** milk glass covered sugar and creamer. Introduced in the 1958 catalog, the S&C appears to have been made to the end of 1959. The set closely resembles a S&C made by Beatty Glass in the early 1900s. These pieces are as heavy as Swirl is delicate. For whatever reason, very few of these sets are ever seen.

No. 6601, Rib.

The **No. 4402, Thumbprint** S&C were shown in the 1958 catalog, and sold as part of a 5-pc Breakfast Set with two shakers. This set had a short lifespan and it is scarce to rare. This is the first time Fenton used the name Thumbprint for a S&C set.

No. 4402, Thumbprint. Courtesy Karen Plott.

The more well known **No. 4403, Thumbprint** was part of the Olde Virginia Glass line from the late 1950s to the early 1960s in milk glass. In 1963, the four transparent colors (amber, olive, blue and pink) were released as part of the general Fenton line. Pink was available through 1968, and the other three colors remained in the catalog until 1969. This is the second S&C set which Fenton called Thumbprint.

No. 4403, Thumbprint.

For two years from 1957-1959, the Fenton catalogs listed the **No. 6901, Teardrop** line. The S&C came only in white milk glass, though other pieces in the line came in colors. The lids are frequently missing from these sugars. Teardrop pieces are thick glass and very heavy.

No. 6901, Teardrop.

The **No. 4301, Lambs Tongue** sugar and creamer has proven to be very elusive. I have asked every S&C collector that I correspond with, two Fenton authors and a Lambs Tongue collector for a photograph, and everyone just shrugs. Someone remembers seeing a pink sugar at a show once, maybe? Lambs Tongue was introduced in the July 1954 supplement, but 6 months later the S&C were not in the 1955 general catalog. Other pieces in the line were produced in white, pink, green and blue pastel milk glass; so the sugar and creamer could have been made in those colors as well.

No. 4301, Lambs Tongue, 1954 catalog supplement.

Introduced in 1961 and discontinued in 1962 was **No. 9100, Jacqueline** S&C. This line was named after the First Lady of the day, Jacqueline Kennedy. Fenton collectors love this set because it's one of the few S&C sets that were produced in the cased-glass known as *Overlay*. Jacqueline comes in Apple Green, Powder Blue, Honey Amber and milk glass.

In 1993, No. 9100 was reissued in cranberry opalescent and cranberry for the FAGCA. The cranberry pieces have a blockier shape to the bowl, in comparison to the softly tapered bowls of the 1961 issue. The newer glass is thicker and the pattern is less finely defined.

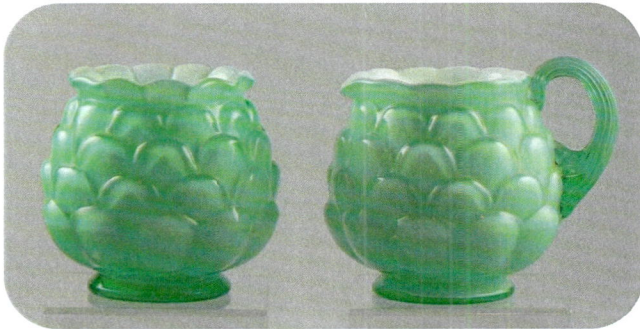
No. 9100, Jacqueline, courtesy Kay & Dave Tucker.

No. 8101, Horizon S&C was only sold through the 1959 catalog supplement. The set did not make it to the 1960 catalog. No. 8101 came in amber, Jamestown Blue and French Opalescent; and just for fun the sugar had a wooden lid. This set is trtp.

8101 FO	Sugar & Cream Set
8162 FO	Oil
8106 FO	Salt & Pepper

No. 8101 Horizon (item D), 1959 catalog supplement.

Cactus in Topaz Opalescent. Courtesy Dick Ladd.

The **Cactus** sugar and creamer was introduced in 1959 in Topaz Opalescent and white milk glass. Topaz Opalescent was discontinued in 1960. This set was sold as **No. 3408** (with a sugar lid) and **No. 3404** (without a sugar lid). This is a cruel joke to play on S&C collectors because we all want the sugar with the lid.

Milk glass Cactus was discontinued in 1961 but was reissued in 1967 as part of the Olde Virginia Glass line. The second time around it was named **Desert Tree** (**No. 3468** creamer and **No. 3488** sugar), and all the sugars were sold with lids. There is no way of knowing whether you have a Cactus or a Desert Tree milk glass set. An amber S&C was also sold under the Desert Tree name. The amber set is scarce and as with most amber transparent glass right now, no one seems to be looking.

The Cactus set was reissued by Fenton in 1974-1975 in Custard Satin. However, instead of being sold as a S&C set, the pieces were sold as the No. 3468 creamer and the No. 3488 candy with lid.

From 1979-1980, blue opalescent, aqua opalescent carnival, and Red Sunset carnival S&C sets were made for Levay Distributing. All the Levay sets had limited production runs and are very difficult to find. A Teal Opalescent set was issued in 1996 which is rare.

The Cactus sugar has been sold as a candy dish in several colors since the 1980s so check your colors before buying an orphan sugar, there may not be a creamer to go with it.

From 1953-1956, Fenton sold the **No. 1903, Daisy & Button,** S&C in milk glass. This was the same mold as the 1930s No. 1900 S&C. No. 1903 is different in that it has a crimped rim. In 1969, the little winged set was sold in the transparent colors of olive, medium blue, amberina and amber. These sets are unmarked and are sometimes mistaken for 1930s issue. In 1973, the set was reissued in white milk glass for the Olde Virginia Glass line. The two issues of milk glass are identical, with the exception of the OVG mark on the later sets. This set has been actively reissued by Fenton with both a crimped and non-crimped rim since the 1980s in various colors.

No. 1903, Daisy & Button.

	Creamer	Sugar w/Lid
#4402 Thumbprint, white	$14	$18
#4403 Thumbprint, amber, olive	$6	$8
#4403 Thumbprint, white	$9	$11
#4403 Thumbprint, blue , pink	$13	$15
#6601 Rib, white	$28	$40
#6901 Teardrop, white	$14	$22
#7006 Swirl, white	$14	$18
#7006 Swirl, blue, pink, green	$25	$31
Cactus, milk or amber	$11	$14
Cactus, custard	$18	$20
Cactus, Topaz Opalescent	$37	$74
Cactus, Blue Opal, Red Carnival	$42	$80
Cactus, Aqua Opal. Carnival	$87	$102
Cactus, Teal Opal	trtp	trtp
	Sugar or Creamer	
#1903 Daisy & Button, amber, olive, white	$8	
#1903 Daisy & Button, amberina, blue	$13	
#9100 Jacqueline, milk, ruby plain	$18	
#9100 Jacqueline, amber	$22	
#9100 Jacqueline, blue or green	$26	
#9100 Jacqueline, ruby opal	$33	

The **No. 5604, Block and Star** set (consisting of the **No. 5661** creamer and the **No. 5627** sugar) was produced in white milk glass from 1955-1957, and in turquoise milk glass during 1955 only. Block and Star is a large heavy set that is oval in shape (when looking down from the top.) The shape and dimensions of this set were copied to the No. 3708 Hobnail S&C shown on the next page.

No. 5604, Block and Star.

No. 3902, Hobnail has a bulbous shape, crown-like rim and two lids. When this set was first introduced in the 1969 supplement, the creamer showed no lid, but by the time the set was released in the 1969 general catalog, both the sugar and creamer had a lid. All the creamers I have examined have a rim for the lid, so I have to wonder if the original, early 1969, creamers had no rim. The set continued with two lids until production ended in the early 1980s.

No. 3902 is easy to find and despite this it retains high popularity with Fenton collectors

No. 3902, Hobnail. Courtesy Karen Plott.

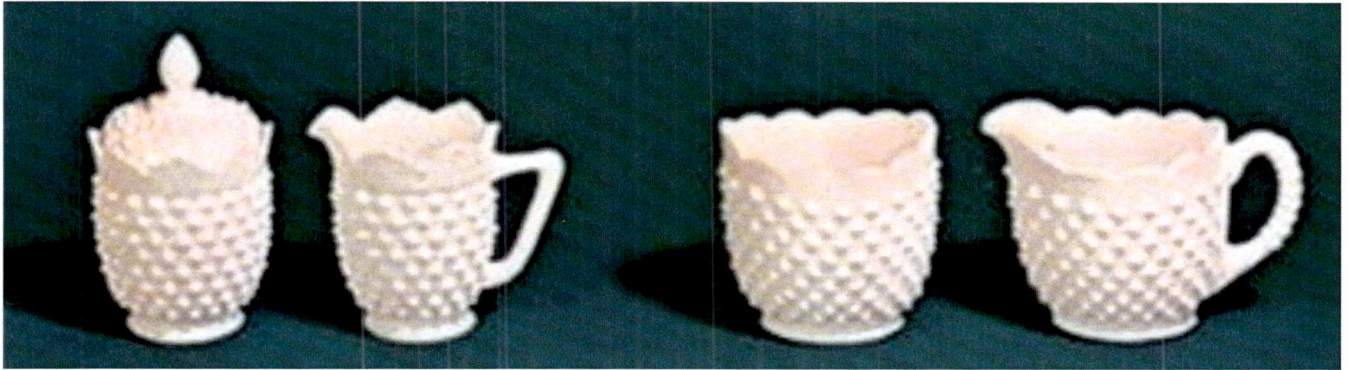

No. 3606, Hobnail next to No. 3708, Hobnail. Size comparison from the 1965 catalog.

The **No. 3606, Hobnail** with its crown-shaped rim is a common set. This milk glass S&C was produced longer than any other Fenton S&C set. Introduced in 1961, No. 3606 had a regular presence in the catalogs for 30+ years. In the 1968 catalog, there was a brief one-year appearance of No. 3606 in crystal. Despite being unusual, collectors ignore these crystal sets.

No. 3606 was reissued in 1980 in Topaz Opalescent for Levay Distributing in very limited numbers. Later in the 1980s, Fenton introduced Sapphire Blue Opalescent and Pink Opalescent as part of the Gracious Touch Home Parties (a Fenton subsidiary). Stiegel Blue Opalescent was sold in 1991 for six months.

I've seen a French Opalescent set but to date I've been unable to determine the year of manufacture.

The **No. 3708, Hobnail** S&C were produced in milk glass from the late 1950s to the late 1960s. The amber version of this set appeared in the Fenton catalogs for 6 months in 1959. This is a large, heavy set which at 5" tall is the same height and oval shape as the No. 5604 Block & Star set.

No. 3665 miniature creamer (left) No. 3708 creamer (right).

The tiny **No. 3702, Hobnail** S&C set has a crimped rim. This set was produced in milk glass in the 1970s. The No. 3665, Hobnail miniature creamer (with straight rim, shown above) was produced as a standalone piece in the 1960s. The two little creamers are easily confused because they have the same height and cylinder shape.

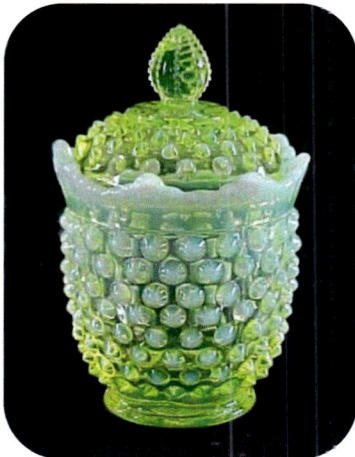

Topaz Opalescent No. 3606. Courtesy Gerri Sorrell.

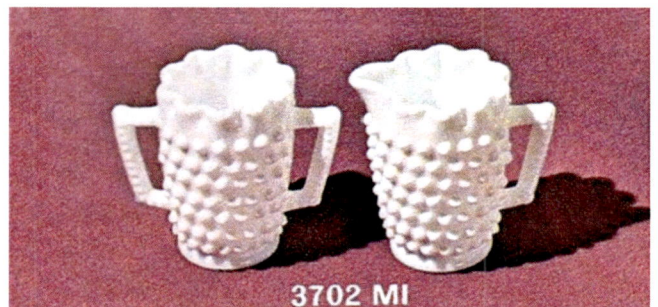

3702 MI

You can find the **No. 9203, Rose** covered S&C in milk glass and transparent colors, as part of the regular Fenton catalogs from 1967-1969. The colors listed in the catalogs were blue, amber and olive. Milk glass continued on in the catalogs until the mid-1970s. Pink was not listed in the general 1967-1969 catalogs, but pink is available to collect and is assumed to be from the same production years. A 1980s reissue was done in iridescent pink.

No. 9203, Rose. Courtesy Vicki Stone.

Talisman Rose was a milk glass line with either yellow or blue painted roses. This was a special order made for the Sears catalog company from March 1969 to September 1970. I've been unable to determine if a blue Talisman Rose S&C was ever made; but I'm beginning to doubt it after asking several Fenton experts. Prices listed are for pieces where the painted roses are in excellent to mint condition. The paint is frequently found faded, as is the case with the creamer below.

Talisman Rose, sold through the Sears catalog.

The **No. 8306, Valencia** sugar and creamer was short-lived. The 3-pc set was made in crystal, amber and olive green, all of which are considered to be some of the least desirable colors to collect right now. Valencia was part of the regular Fenton line from 1970-1972. The Valencia covered candy looks identical to the sugar in photos, so check your measurements because the candy is larger. Valencia sugars are 3" tall and 4 3/8" across the top. In 1988, the sugar and lid were reissued in Blue Opalescent and called a *Trinket Box.*. In 1994, the complete set was reissued in crystal.

No.8306, Valencia.

Hobnail	Creamer	Sugar	Sugar w/lid
#3606 white	$6		$8
#3606 crystal	$8		$11
#3606 French opal	$8		$11
#3606 blue opal	$23		$28
#3606 topaz opal	$30		$36
#3702 white	$5	$5	
#3708 white	$8	$8	
#3708 amber	$10	$10	
#3902 white	$12 *		$12

* Both sugars and creamers have lids

	Creamer	Sugar	Sugar w/lid
#5604 Block & Star, white	$8	$10	
#5604 Block & Star, blue	$13	$16	
#8306 Valencia olive, crystal	$6		$8
#8306 Valencia amber	$8		$10
#9203 Rose amber, olive	$7		$9
#9203 Rose white	$10		$13
#9203 Rose pink, blue	$14		$17
Talisman Rose, yellow	$18		$23

No. 9103, Fine Cut and Block was sold in Cameo Opalescent, crystal and milk glass as part of the Olde Virginia Glass division in the 1970s. Cameo Opalescent is an opal trimmed pinkish-amber glass. After the OVG division closed in 1979, the crystal S&C entered the main Fenton line and was produced into the 1980s. This crystal set is frequently mistaken for the original Fine Cut & Block S&C made in the 1890s. The EAPG set is significantly larger in girth and height. The company re-released this set in Pink Iridescent.

Fine Cut and Block. Courtesy Karen Flott.

In 1974, **No. 8402, Millersburg Cherries (aka Hanging Cherries)** was introduced in amethyst carnival glass. This set closely resembled the original c. 1910 Millersburg Glass creamer and spooner molds. The original Millersburg sugar had a flat rim and a domed lid.

No. 8402, Millersburg Cherries. Courtesy Ruth MacGowan.
In the 1980s, Fenton reissued this set in chocolate glass for Levay Distributing. In the 1990s, the set was made in Rosalene for a home shopping network. Most recently in 2010, Fenton once again resurrected the molds from their archives and sold a red carnival set through their catalog.

From the 1980s and into the new century Fenton continued to produce the occasional sugar and creamer set. Most were made from either old Fenton molds revisited or molds from other glass companies which Fenton had acquired. Some of these sets were made for and sold to a specific audience while others were sold through the gift shop or company catalogs.

From 1982-1984, the **No. 1603, American Legacy** sugar and creamer was made in yellow (Candleglow), olive (Heritage Green), amethyst, and blue (Federal Blue). The narrow necks of some of the hand-finished sugars indicates that the pieces were never intended to actually serve sugar, but were purely decorative.

American Legacy in amethyst (above) and Candleglow (below).

In 1982, Fenton also sold **No. 6300, Flower Band**, which is a tall, footed set with cylinder shaped bowls. There is a molded floral band around the middle of each bowl but beyond that, this set is very plain. The sugars had no handles and the colors available were crystal and light blue. These sets are too rare to price and very few come up for sale.

In 1982, the footed **No. 9503, Strawberry** sugar, creamer, and lid was introduced in crystal. The same set was briefly reintroduced in the mid-1990s in red for a Fenton Collectors Club. The S&C had a design which was similar to an old Cambridge pattern called *Inverted Strawberry*. If you come across a crystal set, with the same strawberry pattern, where the sugar has handles...buy it. It's 100-year-old Cambridge. Fenton sugars don't have handles.

In 2007, the Strawberry S&C was reissued again in Aubergine (amethyst) and a color called Ruby which had undesirable shadings of amberina. This time the set was called **No. 7710, Inverted Strawberry**. The S&C sat on a silly, oversized metal tray which had a winged and naked cherub as the finial. The catalog called these sets, *Antiques of Tomorrow* and the price was as ridiculous as the tray. In 2013, a number of these funky trays were found at the Fenton factory and discounted to online buyers for $34.75 (50% off the original price of $69.50.)

No. 8602, Regency was made from the old McKee Glass **Plytec** molds. From 1986-1990, the open sugar (spooner below) and creamer was made in crystal for the Fenton's *Gracious Touch* home parties. Then in 1988, the complete breakfast set was offered in Topaz Opalescent. These sets are too rare to price and very few come up for sale.

McKee Plytec catalog reprint.

In the late 1990s, Fenton used the individual sized molds from Westmoreland's *Paneled Grape* to create their own version in colors which were never made by Westmoreland. These pieces have the Fenton mark. If you want to own one of these sets, Burmese is the color worth hunting down. It is hard to locate, but quite attractive.

Spiral Ruby Overlay was produced for the 1995 NFGS Convention. Some of the pieces are signed by Fenton family members.

Spiral Ruby Overlay. Courtesy Kay & Dave Tucker.

Topaz Opalescent **Rib Optic** was produced for the 1998 NFGS convention. This set came with the black spoon as shown. With both of these collector-club sets, the creamers will vary in shape from a squat bulb shaped profile (as shown above) to the more hourglass shape (as shown below.) Sugars will also have some variation in shape; but it's the creamers that vary the most.

Topaz Opalescent Rib Optic. Courtesy Lorainne Puskarich.

	Creamer	Sugar
No. 1603 American Legacy, green, yellow	$24	$22
No. 1603 American Legacy, blue, amethyst	$30	$27
No. 8402 Millersburg Cherries, amethyst carnival	$14	$14
No. 8402 Millersburg Cherries, chocolate, Rosalene	$20	$20
No. 9103 Fine Cut and Block, crystal, white with lid	$13	$15
No. 9103 Fine Cut and Block, Cameo Opal with lid	$18	$20
No. 9503 Strawberry, crystal	$12	$15
No. 9503 Strawberry, colors	$19	$25
Spiral Ruby Overlay (+10% for signatures)	$56	$56
Topaz Opalescent Rib Optic (+30% for spoon)	$34	$22

Fostoria's beginning was similar to many other glass houses along the Ohio River. Originally established in the late 19th century, Fostoria was still making glass dinnerware up until they closed their doors in 1986. Most of the pre-Depression Era crystal lines are scarce if not rare, so if you like crystal, purchase these pieces when you see them. There are earlier Fostoria lines known than the ones I start with and undoubtedly, at least some of those lines had S&C sets in them, but catalogs available for public study start in the year 1900, so that's where I start as well. All of these early lines are too rare to price.

No. 501, Hartford Table S&C with spooner. Late 1890s to 1901.

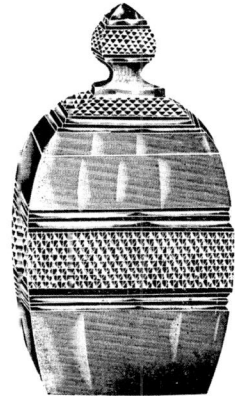

No. 501 1/2, Hartford flat sugar with cover.

No. 601, Diana Table S&C with spooner. Late 1890s to 1913.

No. 675, Edgewood Table S&C with spooner. Late 1890s to 1908.

No. 603, Robin Hood Table S&C with spooner. Late 1890s to 1903.

No. 793, Niagara Table S&C with spooner. 1900-1901.

No. 676, Priscilla is missing the sugar in the catalog illustrations. I created the illustration at left by piecing together elements from the spooner and the butter lid. It's a fantasy creation which shows what the sugar might look like based on the styles of other Fostoria sugars from this time period.

No. 676, Priscilla creamer with spooner. Late 1890s to 1901.

No. 600, Brazilian Table S&C with spooner (above left) and Individual S&C (below left). The size ratio shown between the Table and Individual sets is not indicative of actual sizes.
Late 1890s to 1913.

No. 789, Wedding Bells Table S&C with spooner. Wedding Bells is known in crystal, crystal w/gold on the plain panels, and crystal with flashed rose on the plain panels.

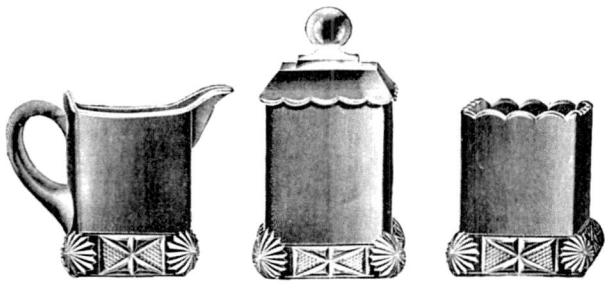

No. 956, Table S&C with spooner. 1901-1903.

*No. 1000, Bedford Table S&C with spooner (above)
and Individual S&C (below). 1901-1904.*

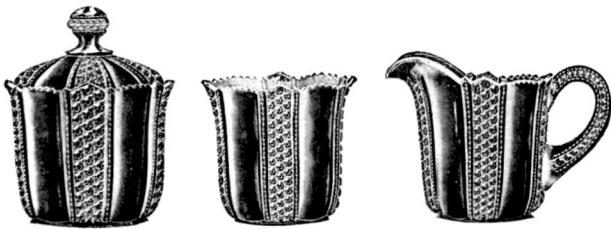

No. 1001, Brilliant Table S&C with spooner. 1901-1904.

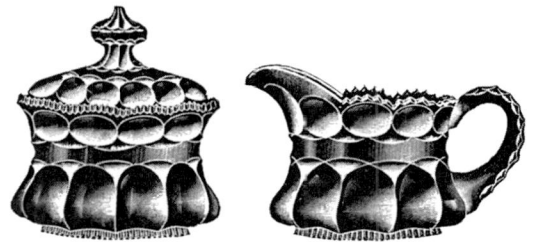

No. 1118, York Table S&C with spooner. 1902-1904.

*No. 1119, Sylvan Table S&C with spooner (above)
and Individual S&C (below). Individual sugar is 3-handled.
1902-1906.*

No. 1121, Louise Table S&C with spooner. 1902-1907.

*No. 1229, **Frisco** Table S&C with spooner. 1903-1905.*

*No. 1299, Table S&C with spooner (above)
and Individual S&C (below). 1904-1913.*

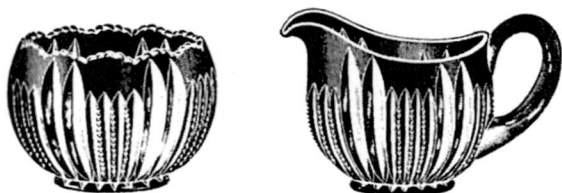

No. 1231, Sugar & Creamer (probably Hotel size). 1903-1908.

No. 1300, Individual Sugar & Creamer. 1904-1906.

No. 1303, Table S&C with spooner. 1904-1925.

No. 1333, Table S&C with spooner. 1905-1913.

*No. 1460, **Old English** Table S&C with spooner. 1906-1908.*

*No. 1467, **Virginia** Table S&C with spooner (above)
and Hotel S&C (below). 1906-1915.
The Hotel set can be found in a marigold carnival finish.*

*No. 1578, **Tuxedo** Table S&C with spooner (above)
and open sugar (below). 1908-1910. The creamer below was not
included on the Fostoria catalog page but I created the illustration to
show what this creamer might look like.*

No. 1641, Table S&C with spooner. 1909-1913.

No. 1578, Tuxedo footed Hotel S&C.

No. 1871, Table S&C with spooner. 1914-1920.

No. 1432, Puritan was a longer running tableware line than most; being in the catalogs from 1906-1925. This is one of the easiest early Fostoria S&C sets for collectors to locate. It can be found plain or with various cuttings.

No. 1432, Puritan Hotel S&C. No other size was made.

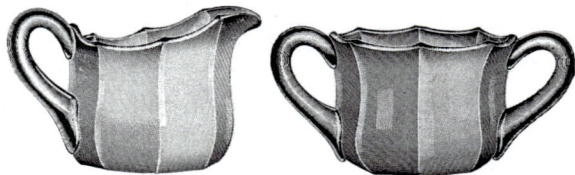

No. 1372. Hotel Sugar.   No. 1372. Hotel Cream.   No. 1372 Spoon.   No. 1372. Sugar.   No. 1372. Cream.

No. 1372, Essex Hotel S&C (above left) and Table S&C with spooner (directly above). 1905-1925.

No. 1515, Lucere Table S&C (direct left) and Individual S&C (directly below). 1907-1915. S&C can be found plain, with gold rim, and with gold painted panel tops. The pieces with the gold panels are part of the *Prince Gold Assortment* (1909-1913).

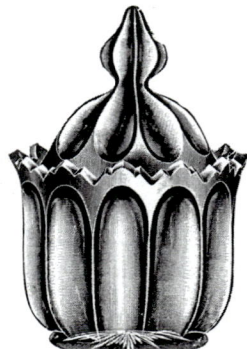

No. 1515 Sugar and Cover   No. 1515 Cream

No. 1515 Ind. Sugar   No. 1515 Ind. Cream

No. 1704 Sugar and Cover   No. 1704 Cream

No. 1704, Rosby Table S&C (left). 1910-1928. Crystal only. In the 1950s, Rosby was reintroduced in white, pink and aqua milk glass under the name of: Winburn. In the 1970s, crystal was again released as part of the Centennial II giftware line.

Note the similar handle shape of all the pieces on this page.

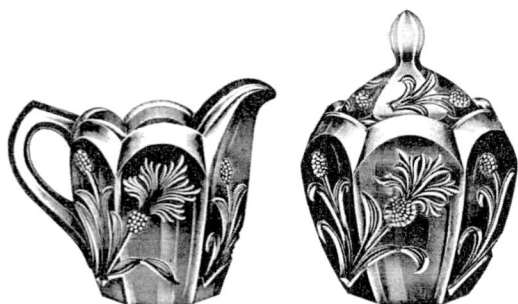

*No. 1819, Table S&C (above) and Hotel S&C (below). Spooner is similar to sugar but has the same narrower profile as the creamer. Collectors call this line: **Dandelion**. 1911-1915.*

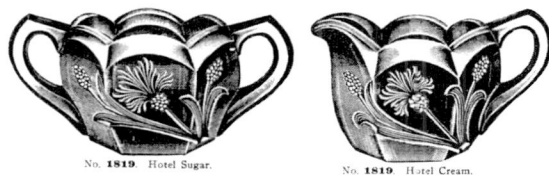

No. **1819**. Hotel Sugar.　　No. **1819**. Hotel Cream.

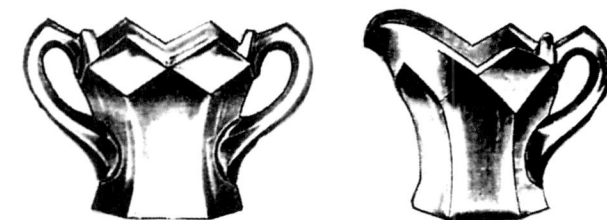

No. 2000, Regal Table S&C (above) and Hotel S&C (below). Spooner is similar to sugar but has the same narrower profile as the creamer. Pieces can be found with cuttings. 1914-1928.

No. 2000 Hotel Sugar　　No. 2000 Hotel Cream
Height 3 inches　Capacity 7 1/2 oz.

The Hotel sized Dandelion and Regal sets are two of the easiest Fostoria S&C sets to locate from the pre Depression era.

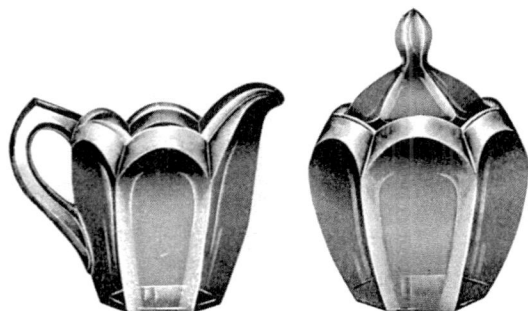

No. 1626, Individual, circa 1914. These pieces are tiny and the sugar may have also been sold as a toothpick. The sharp points on the top damage easily. See the size comparison photo below.

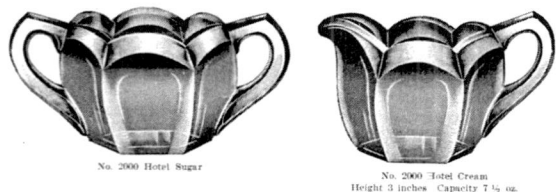

No. 1630, Alexis Table S&C (above) and Hotel S&C (below). Spooner is similar to sugar but has the same narrower profile as the creamer. 1909-1925.

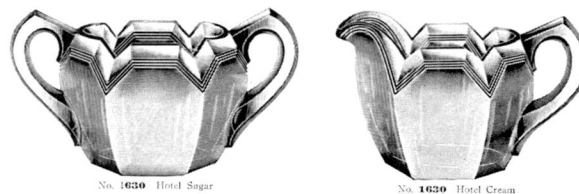

No. **1630** Hotel Sugar　　No. **1630** Hotel Cream

Size comparison between (left to right) Alexis Table creamer (5 inches), Regal Hotel creamer (3 inches), and No. 1626 Individual creamer (2 1/2 inches). All measurements taken at the highest point on the handle. Courtesy Karen Plott.

Below are the three sizes of **No. 2183, Colonial Prism**. Notice the similarities to the Fostoria American shapes which can be found later in this chapter. Colonial Prism was in the catalogs from 1918-1928.

No. 2183, Colonial Prism Table S&C. Sugar height 6 1/4" to top of finial. Creamer height 4". Creamer capacity 10 1/2 oz.

No. 2183 Colonial Prism Hotel S&C. Sugar was sold both with and without the lid. Sugar height 5" to top of finial. Creamer height 2 5/8". Sugar capacity 8 oz. Creamer capacity 6 1/2 oz.
In 1982 the Hotel set (without the lid) was reissued as part of the Colonial Prism Giftware line.

No. 2183 1/2 Colonial Prism S&C. Sugar height 3 1/2" to top of finial. Creamer height 2 2/3". Sugar capacity 9 oz. Creamer capacity 7 oz. Note the lid has no detail while the squat sugar lid shown below does.

No. 2183, squat sugar, sold without a matching creamer.

No. 2106, Vogue Table S&C. Sugar height 5" to top of finial. Creamer height 3". 1916-1929.

No. 2106—English Sugar
Height 3½ inches
Capacity 12 ounces Top Diameter 4⅝ inches

No. 2106½—Hotel Cream
Height 3¼ inches
Capacity 6 ounces

No. 2106 1/2, Vogue English sugar and Hotel creamer.

No. 2106, Vogue had an Individual S&C set which may have stacked. Note how the base of the sugar is nearly as wide as the bowl, while the base of the creamer appears to be small enough to slip down into the top of the sugar. It may not be a coincidence that the butter pat is shown directly above the creamer in the catalogs, indicating that it might have been intended as a lid for the set. The creamer is listed at 4 oz. and the sugar is listed at 5 oz. The 2 3/4" tall Individual sugar was also sold as a standalone piece with a more traditional lid (below left).

Catalogs also show a "Squat" sugar (below right) which stood 2" tall and was sold both with and without a lid. No creamer is shown to accompany the squat sugar. The lid on the Individual and Squat sugars may have been the same lids even though one appears to have a larger finial in the illustrations below.

No. 2106, squat sugar.

No. 1857 Hotel S&C, circa 1915.

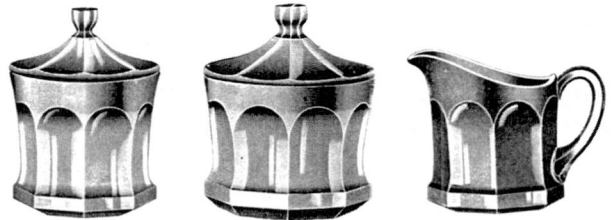

No. 2221½ Sugar and Cover Height, 5¼ inches. No. 2222 Sugar and Cover Height, 5¾ inches. No. 2222 Cream Height, 4 inches. Capacity, 10 ounces.

No. 1913, Flemish Table S&C with spooner (above), and Individual set (below). 1913-1928.

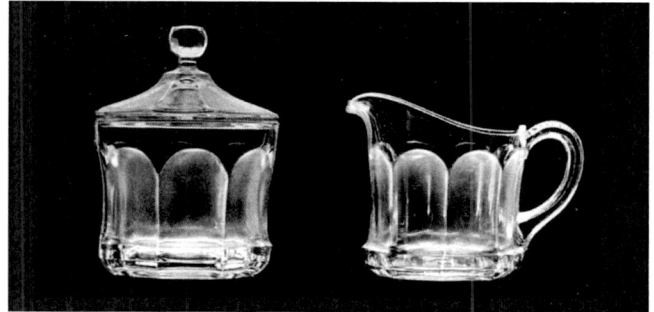

No. 1913 Spoon   No. 1913 Cream

No. 1913 Individual Sugar   No. 1913 Individual Cream

The *No. 2222* Table set (above). The creamer was sold with both a 5 3/4" and a 5 1/4" sugar. The creamer and smaller sugar appeared as a satinized set in one mid-1920s catalog.

The *No. 2222* Hotel S&C (below). The sugar was sold with or without a lid. This creamer bears a striking resemblance to Duncan's No. 61, Hotel creamer.

No. 2222 Hotel Cream Height, 3 inches Capacity, 8½ ounces.   No. 2222 Hotel Sugar Height, 2¾ inches.   No. 2222 Hotel Sugar and Cover Height, 4¾ inches.

In the 1921 catalog, the **No. 1751** Individual sugar was posed alongside a creamer which sat on an underplate (see above). By the mid-1920s, the little sugar got a different creamer as it's companion (see below).

1751 Individual Sugar   1751 Individual Cream

2222-6 oz. Ftd. Oyster Cocktail   2222-Ftd. Individual Cream

The No. 2222 tall footed creamer (above) was displayed in a mid-1920s catalog next to a tall footed oyster cocktail. While, not listed as a set, they may have been sold as such. In 1982, Fostoria reintroduced the creamer with a tall sugar which was identical to the tall oyster cocktail except it had two round handles and was called a sugar.

Prices for all the early Fostoria crystal pieces shown on these pages are similar to the early crystal pieces from other elegant glass companies. If the pieces are identified as *Unknown*, they could price as low as $8-$15 per piece. If the sugar or creamer is correctly identified as Fostoria, that price can go significantly higher. I've seen Rosby, Vogue, and Lucere covered sugars sell in the $40 range and Alexis and Brilliant covered sugars sell in the $50 range. Pieces with cuttings or simple silver overlay sell for slightly more than plain pieces, depending on how elaborate the decoration is. Prices significantly increase on S&C with known Fostoria etchings or elaborate silver overlay decorations.

No. 1861 Spoon   No. 1861 Sugar and Cover   No. 1861½ Spoon

No. 1861 Cream   No. 1861½ Sugar and Cover

*The **No. 1961 & 1961 1/2, Lincoln** Table S&C sets with spooner (above). The 1961 1/2 sugar and spooner have handles. It appears that the same creamer was sold with both sugars. 1912-1928.*

1227 Sugar and Cover, Et. 203   1227 Cream, Et. 203

No. 1227 is a unique shape for Fostoria. The etching shown above (No. 203) was in the catalogs from 1904-1910. Note the etching on the sugar lid. In my opinion, a mint condition set with all three pieces etched, could be the highest priced Fostoria S&C set in this book.

No. 1961, Lincoln Hotel S&C above and below. Note the combination of silver overlay and cuttings which is very desirable on early Fostoria pieces. Photo courtesy Karen Plott.

1911 Fostoria catalog page showing silver overlay decorations.

ILLUSTRATIONS
ARE
REDUCED SIZE

SUGAR AND CREAM SET.
Sugar height, 3⅛ inches; Creamer height, 3¾ inches.
No. 3478/319.................................Per Set $8.00

SUGAR AND CREAM SET.
Sugar height, 2⅛ inches; Creamer height, 3½ inches.
No. 3712/332.................................Per Set $4.00

SUGAR AND CREAM SET.
Sugar height, 2⅜ inches; Cream height, 4 inches.
No. 3159/337.................................Per Set $12.00

SUGAR AND CREAM SET.
Sugar height, 3 inches; Creamer height, 3¾ inches.
No. 3478/351.................................Per Set $8.00

SUGAR AND CREAM SET.
Sugar height, 2⅛ inches; Creamer height, 2¾ inches.
No. 3712/350.................Per Set $4.00

SUGAR AND CREAM SET.
Sugar height, 2½ inches; Creamer height, 2½ inches.
No. 3851/415.................Per Set $18.00
Cut star bottom.

SUGAR AND CREAM SET.
Sugar height, 2¼ inches Creamer height, 3½ inches.
No. 3712/350.................Per Set $4.00

SUGAR AND CREAM SET.
Sugar height, 3⅛ inches; Creamer height, 4 inches.
No. 3478/399.................Per Set $14.00
Cut star bottom.

SUGAR AND CREAM SET.
Sugar height, 3⅛ inches; Creamer height, 4 inches.
No. 3478/391.....................Per Set $8.00

SUGAR AND CREAM SET.
Sugar height, 2⅛ inches; Creamer height, 3½ inches.
No. 3712/390.................Per Set $4.00

SUGAR AND CREAM SET (THREE PIECES).
Sugar height, 2¼ inches; Creamer height, 2¾ inches; Creamer height, 3½ inches.
No. 3712/401 Three-piece Set..........$6.00

SUGAR AND CREAM SET.
Sugar height, 3⅛ inches; Creamer height, 4 inches.
No. 3478/398.................Per Set $11.00
Cut star bottom.

SUGAR AND CREAM SET.
Sugar height, 3⅛ inches; Creamer height, 4 inches.
No. 3478/405.................Per Set $10.00
Cut Star Bottom.

Lookalikes are a reoccurring complication for sugar and creamer collectors. There were certain shapes which repeated between the glass companies; especially in Elegant crystal. In many cases it's difficult or impossible to say for sure if a S&C in one of these shapes is Fostoria, unless it has a confirmed Fostoria decoration. Shown on the previous page is a Fostoria catalog illustration from 1911 showing their versions of some of these popular shapes. Fostoria called the decorating style *Silver Deposit Ware* but collectors typically refer to it as *silver overlay*.

One of the most popular shapes for many of the glass companies was the *hourglass* S&C. Fostoria called their version **No. 1478** in their main catalog and **No. 3478** with silver overlay and it appears that they only made this shape in crystal. No. 1478 came in two varieties. The first had a star cut into the base and the second, had a plain bottom with a polished pontil mark. Those pieces with the cut star originally sold for a higher price.

No. 1478 with No. 45 needle etching (above and below). Sugar is 3 1/8" tall and 3 5/8" across the bottom. Fostoria listed the creamer as being 4" tall. Notice the slight shape variation between the actual sugar and the catalog illustration. Shape variations occur due to different levels of hand work done on individual pieces.

No. 1478 with a rock-crystal type cutting and a cut star in the base.

No. 1478 with all-over silver. Courtesy Karen Plott.

Between the hourglass lookalikes, there is no easy way to tell which company made which S&C, without a confirmed company decoration. However, there are clues to look for: Fostoria pieces either have a pontil mark or a large cut star in their bases. Cambridge pieces are always polished smooth with no pontil mark remaining. Tiffin pieces have either a pontil mark or a molded star in the base. Fry pieces have a pontil mark. Molded stars are centered, cut stars are typically off-center somewhat.

Tiffin creamer spouts have a noticeably tall, pointed profile while the other companies typically have a wide, distinctive curve to their creamer spouts. Tiffin sugar handles almost always extend above the rim of the sugar while Fry, Cambridge and Fostoria typically do not.

Fostoria sugars tend to have the least hourglass shaping, meaning they do not flare out at the top as much as some of the other sugars do. Cambridge creamers tend to be boxy, with less flaring.

Some Fry sets have a pronounced narrow optic. Fostoria, Cambridge, and Tiffin can all have a gentle internal optic.

Other Fostoria hourglass-shaped sets include the **No. 1931** covered sugar and creamer (above as illustrated in the 1910 catalog). Both pieces were listed as having a 5 oz. capacity. That's pretty small, so my guess is these little gems with their flanged tops were considered to be an Individual size.

The **No. 2214** covered sugar and covered creamer (below) had a similar lid and profile to No. 1931, but this sugar was listed at 10 oz. and the creamer at 9 oz., so these were definitely larger than No. 1931. Just looking at these unique rim treatments may make you believe that both of these sets would be easy to spot should you stumble across them. But remember, many sugar and creamer sets have been separated over time and a lidded creamer like this might be mislabeled as a syrup. A lidded sugar might be mislabeled as a mustard or condiment jar.

Shown above is the **No. 1712** sugar and creamer (**No. 3712** with silver overlay), which was sold with and without the sugar lid. These flat bottom, round handled pieces are frequently found with simple cuttings instead of etchings, so they are difficult to distinguish amongst the lookalikes. It both helps and is confusing to know that Fostoria listed the height of the No. 1712 sugar at both 2 1/8" and 2 1/4" tall. So let measurements guide you but not rule you as you try to determine if a set is Fostoria or not. The No. 1712 creamer was listed as 2 1/8".

No. 1712 set with No. 224 etching.

The No. 1712 sugar was also sold with the **No. 1712 1/2** creamer which stood 2 7/8" tall (above) and a third creamer (also known as No. 1712 1/2) which had a stuck handle and stood 3 1/2" tall.

No. 2214 Sugar and Cover,
Etched 253
Capacity 10 ounces
Height 3½ inches

No. 2214 Cream and Cover,
Etched 253
Capacity 9 ounces   Height 3¾ inches

No. 2214 with No. 253, Persian etching.
Sugar is listed as 3 1/2" tall and the creamer is 3 3/4" tall.

No. 3712 set with No. 1712 1/2 tall creamer. Courtesy Karen Plott.

No. 1851 with etching No. 217 (above) and etching No. 264, Woodland (below). Sugar capacity is 8 oz., creamer capacity is 7 1/2 oz.

No. 1851 with cuttings showing the cut star in the base. These stars are frequently off-center while a molded star is always centered.
No. 1851 was known as No. 3851 when it appeared with silver overlay.

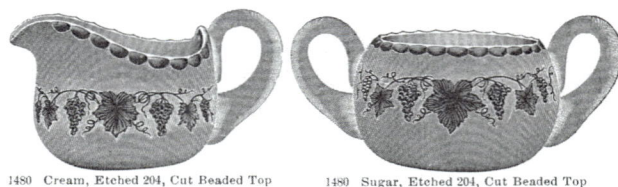

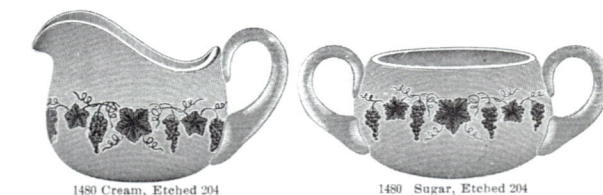

Shown above are two examples of **No. 1851** catalog illustrations. This is a long running Fostoria set which came with enough different etchings that you have a good chance of finding an etched set to call your own. The overall shape is unique enough that it's possible to identify plain crystal sets as Fostoria. Notice between the two illustrations above, the handles are both parallel to the base and slightly angled. Both styles of handle are found and sometimes they are found together as a set.

These sets vary in height from 2 1/8" tall to 2 1/2"; and some have a star cut into the bottom while others have a polished pontil mark. The pieces with the cut star bottoms sold for approximately 30% more than those with the polished pontil mark.

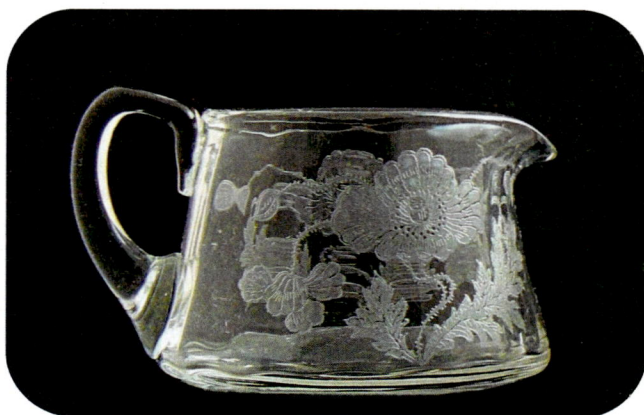

1480 Cream, Etched 204, Cut Beaded Top   1480 Sugar, Etched 204, Cut Beaded Top

1480 Cream, Etched 204   1480 Sugar, Etched 204

The two sets shown above were both known as **No. 1480** in the Fostoria catalogs. Though they have the same line number and etching (No. 204, Vintage), they are slightly different. Notice the differences between the sizes of the leaves and the placement of the curly stems which go upward. I have found these same differences do appear on production pieces, so it isn't just an artists conception. Now notice the handle differences, I have never seen No. 1480 with the large, heavy handles as shown in the top drawing, but that doesn't mean that oversized handles don't exist, so keep your eyes open. If you find these heavy handles, they would be very unusual and unique.

No. 1851 with Rogene etching. Courtesy Kay & Dave Tucker.

No.1480 - Sugar   No. 1480 - Cream

This No. 1480 basic shape was made in crystal by nearly every Elegant Glass company in the 1920s including Westmoreland, Duncan, and McKee. To further complicate the identification, No. 1480 is listed as being made with and without internal optics. You will need to look for a confirmed Fostoria decoration to know for sure if your set is Fostoria.

Fostoria No. 2133 with No. 267, Virginia etching and internal optic.
Photos above and below, courtesy Kay & Dave Tucker.

Cambridge No. 136 (left) and Fostoria No. 2133 (right). Fostoria handles were smaller and placed higher on the glass. The base of the Cambridge handles is a large clump of glass. Fostoria pieces came both with and without an internal optic. While both sugars appear to be about the same height, the Cambridge sugar holds almost 2 more ounces.

No. 2133 was in the catalogs from the late 1910s until the late 1920s and it was sold with different plate etchings, needle etchings and cuttings. Most times the set was shown in the catalogs with no measurements included. Other times conflicting measurements were listed. My creamer measures 3 1/2" tall and holds almost a full 8 oz. My sugar is slightly taller and holds a little over 8 oz.

No. 2133 with No. 250, Oriental etching.
No internal optic, ground bottom.

Fostoria's **No. 2133** (above) and No. **303** (below) appeared in many of the same catalogs during the 1920s. While they look similar in the illustrations, the No. 303 set is significantly larger.

No. 303 is shown above with the No. 53, Parisian needle etching. The set is noted and illustrated as having an internal optic. The sugar size is listed as 3 7/8" with a capacity of 16 oz. That is robust.

A decade later No. 303 appears again in the catalogs and this time it sports a lid and has no optic. The sugar is listed as 5" tall (to the top of the finial) with a capacity of 14 oz. The creamer is listed as 4" tall with a capacity of 15 oz. Perhaps this design change was due to the availability of granulated sugar which allowed consumers to seek out smaller sugar bowls.

No. 303 Sugar and Cover   No. 303 Cream
Cut 129   Cut 129

Whole books have been written about the Fostoria **No. 2056, American** line. American was first introduced in 1915 and pieces remained in the Fostoria catalogs until the company closed in the 1980s. The crystal S&C sets shown on this page are readily available for today's collector. There were three different creamers (Tea, Individual and Large) and four different sugars (Tea, Individual, Large and Large without handles aka *barrel-shaped*). The Tea sized set and the tray were the last to be introduced in 1939. All of these pieces were sold for anywhere from 35 to 65 years.

Size comparison for the three common sugars. From left: Tea, Individual and Large.

2056½—Tea Sugar
Height 2¼ in.

2056½—Tea Cream
Height 2⅜ in.
Capacity 3 oz.

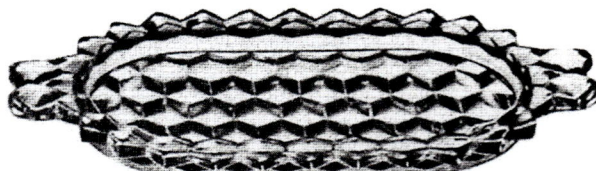

2056—6¾ in. Sugar and Cream Tray
Width 4 in.

2056—Individual Sugar
Height 2½ in.

2056—Individual Cream
Height 2¾ in.
Capacity 4¾ oz.

2056—Sugar and Cover
Height 6¼ in.

2056—Cream
Height 4¼ in.
Capacity 9½ oz.

2056½
Handled Sugar and Cover
Height 5¼ in.

Some of the non-standard American S&C sets are rare and S&C collectors have to compete with a large number of American collectors to add these gems to their collections.

Collectors will sometimes marry the handleless sugar (aka barrel sugar) with the pint pitcher for display in their collections. The pint pitcher is 5 3/8" high. Courtesy Pat & Dennis Early.

Although the Tea-sized sugar and creamer was sold on the 6 3/4" tray (shown previous page), their diminutive size displays nicely on the 8" oval tray. Courtesy Pat & Dennis Early.

Some collectors want to own the hexagonal sugar and creamer set which was primarily sold in England. While this set used to be rare in the US, the advent of online selling has allowed quite a few of these pieces to make their way across the pond and prices have come down dramatically. The hexagonal sugar is 4 1/2" across. Courtesy Pat & Dennis Early.

Individual size with a Sterling base. Courtesy Pat & Dennis Early.

Red flashed Large S&C. Courtesy Pat & Dennis Early.

There are no documented dates for the "Luster" colors but they are believed to have been made in the mid-1920s. Lusters are lightly iridized. The color shown above is known as Autumn Glow. Notice the creamer above has a colored handle while the sugar does not. Below is the large creamer with the Luster treatment.
Both photos courtesy Pat & Dennis Early.

Like the Lusters, there isn't a lot of documentation about the 3-pc. colored S&C sets. The individual set on tray in green, pink, and orchid was probably produced in the 1920s. The 10 1/2" tab-handle tray was the chosen partner for these colored sets. Crystal sets were not sold on this larger tray.

The colored trays are typically more difficult to find than the sugar and creamer themselves. All of these colors are rare, but you will find four green sets for every pink or orchid set out there.
Courtesy Kay & Dave Tucker.

Crystal S&C

In general, Hotel sets are easier to locate than Table sets. Many of the Table sets have disappeared into EAPG collections. Most items shown in this section are too rare to price, but I do have prices on the following:

No. 1432, Puritan, No. 1961, Lincoln, No. 2000 Regal	$8/piece +
No. 1515, Lucere, No. 1819, Dandelion	$12/piece
No. 2183, Colonial Prism	$12/piece
No. 1478, No. 1480, No. 1712	$10/piece +
No. 2133	$15/piece +

+ Add 20% for simple cuttings or silver overlay, 50% for elaborate cuttings or needle etchings, 2x for silver with cuttings, 2x-3x for etchings, 3x for all over silver and silver with etchings.

American	Crystal	Green	Red Flashed
Tea sugar or creamer	$7		
Individual sugar or creamer	$5	$70	
Large, sugar with handles / lid	$17		
Large sugar no handles / lid	$22		
Large creamer	$10		$25
Tray, 6 3/4" saw-tooth handle	$15		
Tray, 6" tab-handle	$30		
Tray 10" tab-handle		$80	
English Hexagonal sugar	$120		
English Hexagonal creamer	$120		
All other colors, finishes and variations are trtp.			

Confusion exists between the many different S&C which have a cube pattern. In particular, there is a small cubed sugar and creamer shape which was made by both Hazel-Atlas and Jeannette which is frequently misidentified as American. Further ahead in the Hazel-Atlas chapter, these little lookalikes are discussed in depth. But if you are still confused, look at the handles. American's round handles allow it to stand out amongst the lookalikes.

Indiana Whitehall. Courtesy Pat & Dennis Early.

There also exists some confusion with the crystal Indiana **Whitehall** set shown above. Whitehall was produced from the 1960s into the 1980s and the S&C are similar in size to the large American S&C set.

Philip Ebeling, the primary designer of the American line, also designed the **Cube** line for the Jeannette Glass company. Jeannette pieces have such a different profile and handles that there really shouldn't be any confusion with the American line.

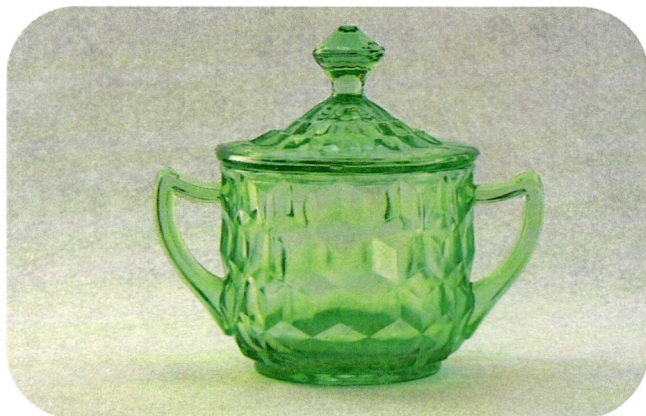

Jeannette Cube sugar with lid.

The little known **No. 1759** set had a presence from the 1910s into the early 1920s. This crystal S&C is one of those sets which could be easily lost to collectors because if the pieces were split up the sugar could be sitting alone somewhere labeled as a sherbet.

No. 1759 with No. 212 etching.

1925 was the year Fostoria began to sell colored glass in earnest. One of the earliest colored S&C sets available was **No. 2315**. Originally sold with a tall creamer that resembled No. 1759, the set came in crystal, Vaseline, blue, amber and green. The tall creamer was made for only two years.

In 1927 the catalogs show the No. 2315 1/2 squat creamer. The squat creamer came in the additional colors of orchid and pink. Both of the No. 2315 sets can be found decorated with metal and cuttings.

No. 2315 in Orchid with unknown silver overlay.

No. 2315 with Wheeling Class D-53 decoration.

Another early colored S&C was the spiraled **No. 2255**. This pair was not part of a larger tableware line and was sold as a standalone set. Originally sold in amber, Azure and green, pink was later added. Azure blue is the most difficult to find.

No. 2315 sugar with No. 2315 creamer (top row) and No. 2315 1/2 creamer (bottom row). Plain amber sets like this were sold through the 1927 Sears catalog.

No. 2255. Sugar. (Made in Amber, Blue and Green only)   No. 2255. Cream. (Made in Amber, Blue and Green only)

No. 2255. Mid to late 1920s.

No. 2321, Priscilla causes some confusion with collectors. The S&C were originally introduced in 1925 in crystal, amber, green and blue. Blue was discontinued after two years. Later, Azure (light blue) and pink were added to the color lineup. This makes Priscilla the only Fostoria S&C set which can be found in both Azure and blue.

At some point Fostoria made the decision to release the sugar and creamer on a tray. Unfortunately, the sugar was too large for the tray, so instead they sold a set which included the flared bouillon bowl, not the sugar. You can collect the actual S&C or you can collect the 3-piece set.

No. 2321 bouillon (left) next to sugar (right) for comparison.

No. 2321, Priscilla 3-pc set above and below.
Photo courtesy Karen Plott.

No. 2350, Pioneer was Fostoria's first big colored dinnerware line. Introduced in 1926 there were two different S&C sets to chose from. Both sets were sold in multiple colors and with etchings. Pioneer has a distinctive tiny knob at the top of the handle where it meets the bowl.

Nos. 2350 (flat) and 2350 1/2 (footed), Pioneer S&C.

No. 2350, the flat Pioneer S&C was made in crystal, amber, green, and blue and sold with or without the lid. No. 2350 1/2, the footed set came in crystal, amber, green, blue, pink, black and red. Red is the most difficult color to find. The footed set can also be found with a wide variety of decorations done by Fostoria and multiple outside decorating companies.

Colors and the flat set were discontinued in the mid-1930s but the footed crystal S&C were in Fostoria's line-up well into the 1950s. The rare lid for the footed set (next page) appears to have only been made in crystal, amber and green.

No. 2350 1/2, Pioneer footed S&C. The red of this set is slightly orangish in hue. The color is of high quality, tightly controlled and without much variance. Lookalikes with poorly controlled reds that vary in hue, are too dark, or that "gather" need not be confusing.

Pioneer is one of only a few S&C sets made in red during the Depression era. If you find any of these red sets and the price is reasonable, you should buy them when you can.

No. 2350, Pioneer in blue with Vesper etching on sugar, creamer and lid. Courtesy Karen Plott.

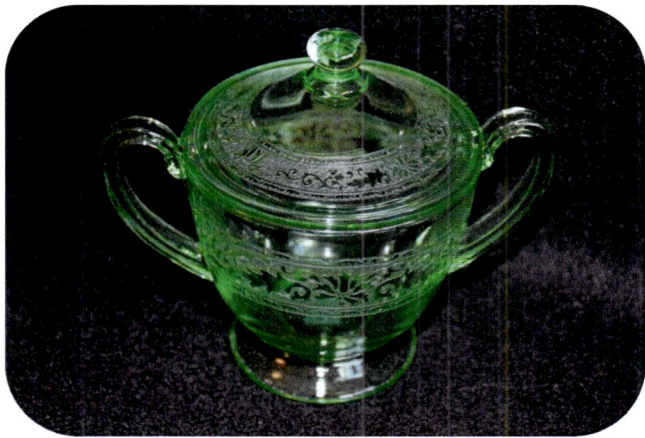

No. 2350 1/2, Pioneer with Vesper etching on sugar and lid. Lids for the footed sugars are rare. Courtesy Dick Ladd.

No. 2350 1/2, Pioneer S&C with Rockwell Silver overlay in the "Fawn" decoration. Courtesy Dick Ladd.

Pioneer sugar with lid (below left) next to Fairfax sugar with lid (below right). While nearly identical, the Fairfax lid has subtle ribbing whereas the Pioneer lid is smooth. Courtesy Karen Plott.

No. 2375, Fairfax was the most successful colored dinnerware for Fostoria from the late 1920s and throughout the 1930s. There were four different sugars and three different creamers in the line. All of the sets came in crystal, green, amber and Orchid. In addition, the tall footed set came in pink, Azure, yellow, and Mother-of-Pearl. The Tea-sized S&C added black and red to the roster. The Tea-sized red S&C are scarce. The color Orchid was only made from 1927 to 1928.

In general, Fairfax pieces are known by their subtle external ribs and slight points on their rims. The No. 2375 set was in the catalogs through 1932, and the two No. 2375 1/2 sets were in the catalogs until the early 1940s. Catalogs show the full sized No. 2375 ½ sugar was sold with and without a lid.

The fourth, and most mysterious sugar is an uncommonly found flat-rimmed piece which is frequently mistaken for a Pioneer sugar. Unlike Pioneer, this piece does have the typical external ribbing. It seems logical that a flat-rimmed sugar in a family of pointed-rim pieces would have been made to sit under a lid. However, all the lids I've been able to examine look slightly undersized when placed on this sugar. In comparison, the lids fit the pointed-rim sugar very well. The flat-rimmed sugars are slightly larger in diameter than the pointed rim sugars and there may be two sizes of lid out there. Without a catalog reference to cite, the flat-rimmed sugar remains an enigma.

No. 2375, flat Fairfax in Orchid.

No. 2375 1/2 footed Fairfax S&C; 3 1/2" high with 6 1/2 oz. capacity and No. 2375 1/2 Tea-sized Fairfax S&C (frequently called Individual); 2 1/2" high with 3 oz. capacity.

Some unusual colors and finishes to locate, from left to right: Orchid, satinized crystal with silver overlay, and Mother-of-Pearl. The Mother-of-Pearl treatment was done by Fostoria for 10+ years, but S&C are few and far between. Photo courtesy Karen Plott.

Some of the Tea-sized sets are found with a satin and silver decoration sitting on what appears to be a Heisey tray. This would indicate that this decoration was probably done by an outside decorating company. Photos courtesy Frederick Schwartz.

Compare the five sugars above. From left to right are: New Martinsville's point-rimmed sugar (red) Fostoria Fairfax (Azure), Fostoria Fairfax flat rim (pink) Fostoria Pioneer (blue) Central Mimi (green). The New Martinsville sugar is frequently misrepresented as red Fairfax but the handles don't have a groove and the red isn't as well controlled as Fostoria's red (see Fostoria Pioneer section). If you are still a non-believer note that the New Martinsville S&C are also found in their jade-green color and Fostoria did not make a jadite color. Notice the slightly wider diameter of the pink Fairfax in comparison to the Azure Fairfax. The Central piece has distinctive internal wide optic panels.

Nos. 2375 1/2, Fairfax sugars for size comparison.

No. 2429, Service Tray with No. 2429, Lemon Tray insert and No. 2375 1/2 S&C. Set available in crystal, amber, green, pink, yellow and Azure. Courtesy David Lippert, photographer Brad Struna.

The **No. 2419, Mayfair** line had three sizes of sugar and creamer. Both of the larger sets came in crystal, pink, green, amber and yellow. The tiny Tea set additionally came in cobalt, amethyst, dark green, red, black, and the chameleon color of Wisteria.

All of the colors and all of the sizes were introduced in the early 1930s. The round footed set was the first to be discontinued in 1937. The other two sets were discontinued in the early 1940s. Various colors were picked up and dropped at various times with red having the shortest run.

The round sugar stands 3 1/4" tall, the octagonal based, tall sugar stands 3 1/2" tall and the Tea sugar stands 2 3/4" tall. All three sizes can be found with etchings but these are scarce to rare.

There is no catalog proof that the tall Mayfair sugar and creamer was sold with the No. 2419 Condiment tray but in today's market, these three pieces are sometimes found together.

Buried on a Miscellaneous catalog page with a fuzzy drawing is the **No. 2497 1/2** *Fish* S&C. Sugars were also sold as Seafood Cocktails. Colors available were crystal, satinized crystal, cobalt, red, dk. green, and amethyst. Some of the pieces were stretched and made into fish-faced *Swung* vases. Mid to late 1930s.

Courtesy Louis Lopilato.

Fostoria	Crystal	Amber	Yellow	Pink	Green	Other
#2255, sugar or creamer		$8		$9	$12	$24 (blue)
#2315, squat sugar or creamer	$6 *	$6 *		$14 *	$14 *	$16 * (blue) / trtp (Vaseline or Orchid)
#2315, tall creamer	$6 *	$6 *		$20 *	$17 *	$25 * (blue) / trtp (Vaseline)
#2321, Priscilla sugar or creamer	$5	$6		$10	$7	$15 (Azure or blue)
#2321, Priscilla bouillon	$5	$6		$10	$7	$15 (Azure or blue)
#2000, Priscilla tray		$10		$26	$18	$28 (Azure) / $35 (blue)
#2350, Pioneer lid for flat sugar ****	$10 *	$15 *		$20 *	$20 *	$38 * (blue)
#2350, Pioneer flat sugar or creamer	$5 *	$7 *		$9 *	$8 *	$14 * (blue)
#2350 1/2, Pioneer lid for footed sugar ****	$20 *	$24 *			$35 *	$60 * (blue)
#2350 1/2, Pioneer footed sugar or creamer **	$5 *	$6 *		$12 *	$14 *	$16 * (blue) / $15 (black) / $22 (red)
#2375, Fairfax flat sugar or creamer	$5	$6			$9	$12 (Orchid)
#2375 1/2, Fairfax lid for footed sugar ****	$10 *	$12 *	$20 *	$18 *	$16 *	$25 * (Azure) / $50 * (Orchid)
#2375 1/2, Fairfax footed sugar or creamer **	$5 *	$6 *	$8 *	$8 *	$8 *	$10 * (Azure) / $12 * (Orchid)
#2375 1/2, Fairfax Tea sugar or creamer	$5	$6	$8	$7	$7	$10 (Azure) / $12 (black) / $24 (red)
#2429, Fairfax Service tray ****	$15 *	$20 *	$36 *	$20 *	$24 *	$52 * (Azure)
#2429, Fairfax Lemon tray	$12	$16	$24	$16	$20	$40 (Azure)
#2419, Mayfair round sugar or creamer ***	$5 *	$6 *	$9 *	$9 *	$9 *	
#2419, Mayfair tall sugar or creamer ***	$5	$8	$8	$12	$12	
#2419, Mayfair Condiment tray			$30	$42	$34	
#2419, Mayfair Tea sugar or creamer ***	$5	$6 *	$7 *	$10 *	$10 *	$10 (black and dk. green) / $12 (amethyst and cobalt) $16 (wisteria) / $25 (red)
#2497 1/2, Fish sugar or creamer	$12 (clear or satinized)					$25 (dk. Green and amethyst) / $32 (cobalt and red)

* Any decorated piece might price higher. Pieces with common silver overlay, add 20%, pieces with unusual silver overlay, add 50-300%. Pieces with simple cuttings, add 20%. Pieces with elaborate cuttings or cuttings with metal, add 50%. Etched pieces price 3x-4x depending on desirability and scarcity.

** Fairfax sugars with flat rims price 25-30% higher than pointed rim sugars.

*** Etched Mayfair S&C price up to 2x the price listed for undecorated pieces.

**** Etched sugar lids and Service trays price 4x-5x the price for undecorated pieces.

The **No. 2440, Lafayette** sugar and creamer with their curled handles is one of the most readily recognized and beloved Fostoria S&C sets. Lafayette was sold from the 1930s into the 1980s and crystal pieces are common. Even some of the etched crystal sets are common as they were produced for 20+ years.

Colored Lafayette sets are available in pink, green, amber, yellow, Wisteria, cobalt, amethyst and dark green. Wisteria seems to be the most beloved color but dark green is proving to be the most difficult to find. This set was not made in red by Fostoria for some reason, but recently Fenton has reproduced the creamer in red. All of the colors can be collected at a reasonable price with a little patience.

The tray which was sold with Lafayette went by **No. 2470**. Trays came in crystal, green, yellow, amber and pink. Fostoria sold the crystal tray with the Florentine, Morning Glory and Flemish etchings and the yellow tray with the Florentine etching. These etched trays are rare. Should you find one, buy it and look for the matching sugar and creamer later.

No. 2440, Lafayette sugar and creamer on No. 2470 tray with No. 319, Flemish etching. Courtesy Jean & Vic Laermans.

No. 311 Florentine etching. Courtesy Jean & Vic Laermans.

No. 2449, Hermitage was made in the mid-1930s in crystal, yellow, amber, green, red and Wisteria. Then in 1974 the line was reissued for one year under the line name of **Lexington**. The new colors were olive green, brown and yellow. I've been unable to determine if the early and later yellows are the same shade.

Yellow is the easiest color to find with Wisteria and red being the most difficult. Collectors virtually ignore crystal, amber, brown and olive green.

Wisteria Hermitage under artificial light (above) and natural light (below). Photos courtesy Kay & Dave Tucker.

No. 2449, Hermitage and Lexington. From left to right: brown, amber and yellow.

Fostoria gave three different line numbers to the same sugar and creamer blank. **No. 4020** is the designation for solid crystal. **No. 4120** designates the sets with the crystal bowls and colored feet. **No. 4220** is the number for the pieces with the pink and yellow bowls. This is a fun family to collect because it has some of the favorite things that S&C collectors enjoy: etchings and multiple colors to hunt down.

No.4120 with No. 285, Minuet etching. Courtesy Jean & Vic Laermans.

No. 4120 with No. 501, Fern etching. Courtesy Kay & Dave Tucker.

No. 4120 with No. 306, Queen Anne etching. Courtesy Jean & Vic Laermans.

No. 4120 with Wisteria base. Courtesy Karen Plott.

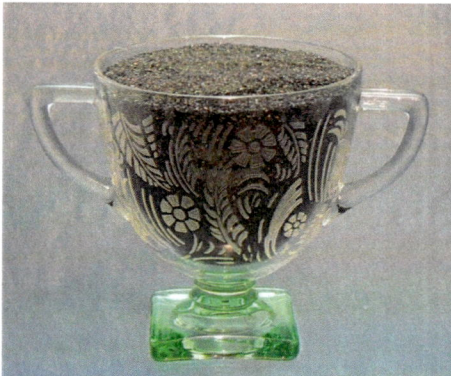
No. 4120 with No. 283, Kashmir etching. (Black sugar used to highlight etching).

No. 4220 with No. 284, New Garland etching. Courtesy Jean & Vic Laermans.

No. 4220 pink bowl with crystal base.

Fostoria	Crystal	Amber	Yellow	Pink	Green	Other
#2440, Lafayette sugar or creamer	$5 *	$7	$8 *	$10	$10	$14 (dk. green and amethyst) / $18 (cobalt and Wisteria)
#2470, tray	$8 *	$10	$11 *	$12	$15	
#2449, Hermitage sugar or creamer	$5	$6	$9		$18	trtp (Wisteria and red)
#2449, Lexington sugar or creamer	$6 (brown)		$9		$8 (olive)	
#4020, sugar or creamer	$7 +					
#4120, sugar or creamer colored base		$9 +			$11 +	$14 + (black) / $18 + (Wisteria)
#4220, sugar or creamer colored bowl			$11 –	$15 +		

* Crystal with etchings price 2x-5x depending on scarcity of etching. Crystal with mass produced etchings from 1940-80 price 2x plain crystal. Etched yellow pieces are trtp.
+ Etched pieces price 2x-3x depending on the desirability of the etching. Fern and Kashmir are two of the most desirable.

Beginning in the mid-1930s, Fostoria introduced a series of dinnerware lines that all had a large S&C and an Individual S&C which sat on a tray. The vast majority of these pieces were made in plain crystal but there are some interesting variations to collect.

No. 2496, Baroque Large and Individual S&C sets.

The **No. 2496, Baroque** sugar and creamer sets are a collector favorite and I would venture to say that every S&C collector who includes Fostoria in their collection, owns at least two sets. Crystal was made for 30 years and the Azure and yellow sets were made for seven years in the 1930s. Just to make your life interesting, Fostoria changed the formula for their Azure in mid-stride and you will find two different shades of blue.

Two different shades of Azure blue. Courtesy Jean & Vic Laermans.

There are many decorations which can be found on the crystal sets; and crystal pieces were sold to outside decorating companies.

Both sizes of Azure baroque are found with two different etchings: No. 328, Meadow Rose, and No. 329, Lido. Etched Azure sets are not easy to find but the Azure tray with Lido etching is rare. If you find one, buy it and worry about locating a sugar and creamer later. There is no Azure tray with Meadow Rose that I'm aware of.

*One of the etchings found on Baroque is **No. 514, Italian Lace**. It is an all over pattern with a brocade style. Italian Lace came with and without the gold trim. Only the large set is available.*

No. 2496, Individual Baroque with height, capacity and tray detail.

No. 2510, Sunray sets were in the catalogs from the mid-1930s until 1943. The tray for the individual set looks much like the Baroque tray. Both sizes can be found with satinized ribs and the satinized pieces were known as **Glacier.**

No. 2510, large Sunray with Glacier decoration. Courtesy Dan Tyner.

No. 2510, Individual Sunray set with unknown silver overlay.

No. 2560, Coronet was made from 1938-1959 in crystal. Two of the more readily found etchings on this set are No. 332, Mayflower and No. 333, Willowmere. A few trays were etched and these can be a challenge to find.

Large Coronet sugar with No. 332, Mayflower etching and creamer with No. 333, Willowmere etching.
Individual Coronet with Mayflower etching below.

2560—3 Piece
Ind. Sugar and Cream and Tray

No. 2560, Individual Coronet showing tray detail.

Available from 1939-1969 was the **No. 2574, Raleigh** S&C in two different sizes. It was a design with large open spaces ideal for decorating. Raleigh was the canvas for two scenery-type etchings, No. 335 Willow and No. 336, Plymouth. Willow is significantly easier to find than Plymouth. Raleigh blanks were also sold to outside decorating companies. As far as I've been able to determine, no Raleigh trays were etched.

No. 2574, Raleigh Individual showing tray detail.

Large No. 2574, Raleigh with No, 335 Willow etching.

The **No. 2412 Colony** line was in the catalogs for 30 years from 1940-1970. The large S&C set was reissued in crystal and red in the 1980s.

No. 2412, large Colony S&C reissued in red for Christmas 1981-1982.

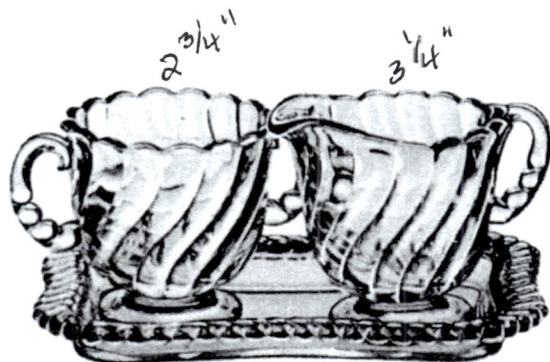

2412—Ind. Sugar and Cream and Tray
Height 3½ in.

*No. 2412, Colony Individual S&C showing tray detail (above)
and large S&C (below).*

2412—Footed Sugar
Height 3⅜ in.

2412—Footed Cream
Height 3⅞ in.

No. 2630, Century was introduced in 1949 with the familiar formula of two sizes and a tray. Century sets were made for 25 years and are readily available. The decorated sets with the matching etched trays are the most desirable and unlike other Individual trays, the Century decorated trays aren't too difficult to find. Two of the more unusual decorations to find are: Lacy Leaf and Milkweed. These were crystal prints (which are similar to etchings but not as heavy). Both of these designs were only done for one year.

No. 2630, Century large S&C with No. 345 Starflower etching.

Individual Century with Milkweed crystal print, showing tray detail.

#2496 Baroque	Crystal	Yellow	Azure
Sugar or creamer, large	$5 +	$8	$10 +++
Sugar or creamer, small	$7 +	$12	$12 +++
Tray	$7 ++	$14	$16 +++
Fostoria			**crystal**
#2412 Colony, Individual sugar or creamer			<$5
#2412 Colony, large sugar or creamer			<$5
#2412 Colony, large sugar or creamer, red			$14
#2412 Colony, tray			$6
#2510 Sunray, Individual sugar or creamer			$7 +
#2510 Sunray, large sugar or creamer			$9 +
#2510 Sunray, tray			$8 ++
#2560 Coronet, Individual sugar or creamer			$6 +
#2560 Coronet, large sugar or creamer			$8 +
#2560 Coronet, tray			$15 ++
#2574 Raleigh, Individual sugar or creamer			$5 +*
#2574 Raleigh, large sugar or creamer			$5 +*
#2574 Raleigh, tray			$15
#2630 Century, Individual sugar or creamer			$5
#2630 Century, large sugar or creamer			<$5
#2630 Century, tray			$6 ++

+ Some etchings are significantly more common than others. Shop around and compare. If an etching was done for 10+ years price at 50% higher than plain. Less common etchings start at 2x the price of plain. Post 1950 silver overlay price at +50%, earlier silver overlay 2x. Add 25% for Glacier decoration.
++ All etched trays start at 2x plain crystal. A few etchings are more expensive depending on availability. Shop around and compare. Fostoria etchings can be grossly overpriced. Silver decorated Sunray trays are 2x. Glacier trays are 2x.
+++ Etched Azure large S&C price 3x plain Azure, Individual S&C price at 4x. Etched Azure trays are trtp.
* Willow etching is readily available, Plymouth is scarce.

No. 2620, Wistar was a short-lived line of crystal occasional pieces in the early 1940s. There was only one size of sugar and creamer and no tray. The S&C were reissued in milk glass in the 1950s and renamed, **Betsy Ross**. Because of this name change, the crystal S&C are more often than not referred to as Betsy Ross.

2620—Footed Sugar
Height 3½ in.

2620—Footed Cream
Height 4 in.
Capacity 7½ oz.

In 1954, Fostoria introduced No. 1704, **Winburn,** which was made from the old No. 1704, Rosby molds from the 1920s. White milk glass Winburn sets were sold until the mid-1960s. The milk glass market proved to be successful enough for Fostoria that they tried their hand at aqua and pink milk glass. At this same time, Fenton was also dipping their toe into pink and blue milk glass to see if there was a steady market for it. The experiment wasn't a huge success for either company and the pastel colors were only in Fostoria catalogs from 1957-1959.

*Vintage (no known line number). Made in white from 1958-1965. The Vintage tray is the same tray that was sold with the **No. 2712 Berry** S&C. Courtesy Karen Plott.*

No. 2712, Berry set with tray. Made in white from 1957-1965. Courtesy Brandon Dowd.

No. 1704, Winburn. Courtesy Karen Plott.
Note: Rosby was rereleased in lead crystal in the 1970s.

No. 2711, Diamond Starburst. Made in white from 1957-1965. This set is occasionally found on the tray which was sold with the Vintage and Berry sugar and creamer sets (see above), but this set was not sold with a tray. However, I'm all for enjoying your glass and if your set is on a tray and you like it, then please keep it that way. Courtesy Karen Plott.

No. 2710, Daisy & Button with tray. Made in white from 1957-1965. This S&C was reissued in lead crystal as part of Fostoria's giftware lines during the mid to late 1970s. The tray was not reissued. The molds for the S&C were acquired by Fenton and later sold by them in crystal and colors. Look for the Fenton mark.

No. 2675, Randolph was made in white from 1955-1965. Occasionally there is confusion between it and an EAPG opaque S&C made by the Atterbury Glass Company. In both the photos directly above and below Fostoria's Randolph is on the left and the Atterbury piece is on the right. Fostoria pieces have a narrower band at the top of the grooves and they are significantly smaller.

Both Atterbury comparison photos courtesy Lora Jo Davis.

Milkglass	White	Pink	Aqua
#1704, Winburn, sugar with lid	$16	$26	$26
#1704, Winburn, creamer	$10	$13	$13
#2620, Betsy Ross, sugar or creamer	$7 *		
#2675, Randolph, sugar with lid	$15	$30	$30
#2675, Randolph, creamer	$8	$12	$12
#2710, Daisy & Button, sugar or creamer	$5 *	$12	$14
#2710, Daisy & Button, tray	$10	$16	$18
#2711, Diamond Starburst, sugar or creamer	$5	$8	$9
#2712, Berry, sugar or creamer	$7	$10	$12
Vintage, sugar or creamer	$7	$14	$14
Vintage / Berry tray	$9	$16	$18

* #2620, Wistar, crystal price < $5,   #687/688 Daisy & Button, crystal price $10

HAVE SUGAR EA.

No. 2666, Contour was first issued in plain crystal. Later the same S&C were sold in opalescent pink and blue under the name of: **No. 2685, Seascape**. The crystal sets are found with various decorations and metal rims. Contour sets were made for 20 years beginning in the 1950s and the Seascape sets were made from 1954-1957.

No. 2685, Seascape (above and below). Notice the different level of opalescence between the pink sugar and the creamer. Sets where all pieces have matching levels of opalescence are most desirable.

One of Fostoria's most popular later patterns is **No. 1372, Coin.** Coin was produced from 1958 until the early 1980s. After Fostoria closed their doors, Lancaster Colony purchased the molds and Coin was reissued. Fostoria Coin items have satinized coins while Lancaster Colony items have clear coins.

The covered sugar and creamer came in crystal, amber, olive green, aqua, red and an emerald green. The emerald set was only made for two years, and it's the most difficult to find. The original aqua S&C were made from 1963-1966. From 1975-1982, Coin items were made in a different, more bluish shade of aqua but I have never seen a S&C in this color. The unusual amethyst sets which are found appear to be sun damaged crystal which has been artificially accelerated.

Coin	Creamer	Sugar with lid
Crystal (American)	$5	$8
Crystal (Canadian)	$22	$35
Amber or Olive green	$7	$12
Aqua	$17	$24
Red	$10	$15
Emerald green	$30	$48

Note: Clear coins are post-1983 and price 25-50% less than frosted coins

No. 2650, Horizon was in the catalogs from 1951-1954. The sugar and creamer came in Cinnamon and Spruce Green. This is a heavy, chunky set that collectors are in no hurry to purchase.

No. 2650, Horizon in Cinnamon.

No. 1372, Coin in Emerald green. Courtesy Kay & Dave Tucker.

In the mid-1960s, Fostoria issued some crystal Coin items to commemorate the Canadian Centennial. The frosted coins had a bobcat, wolf, bird and goose embossed on them.

No. 1372 with Canadian coin decoration.
Courtesy MAGWV, photographer Bob O'Grady.

No. 4186, Mesa is a small line of miscellaneous tableware items with a thumbprint motif. The covered sugar and creamer was made in crystal, olive green, brown, amber and blue. Mesa was in the catalogs from 1968-1970. There isn't a lot of Mesa available to purchase but because today's collector isn't wild about the earth tones which were so popular in the 1960s, the only color which seems to be in demand is blue.

No. 4186, Mesa. Courtesy Karen Plott.

No. 2718, Fairmont was a small tableware line with only nine items for sale. Production was from 1960-1965 and the available colors were crystal, amber, blue and green. Considering the length of time this pattern was made, the set is harder to find than it should be.

Note the differences between the Fairmont catalog drawing (above) and the actual S&C (below).

No. 2718, Fairmont.

No. 2719, Jamestown came in crystal, blue, green, amber, pink, amethyst and brown. Most of the colors were introduced in the late 1950s, with pink and brown being introduced in 1961. All of the colors remained in the catalogs until 1973, except for amethyst which was discontinued in 1965. With some perseverance, all of the colors can be collected.

No. 2719, Jamestown.

No. 2806, Pebble Beach was available in Black Pearl, Lemon Twist, Pink Lady, Mocha, and crystal. Manufactured only in 1969, this set is scarce in any color and if you like it, you should pick it up when you see it.

No. 2806, Pebble Beach in Lemon Twist.

The **No. 2770, Argus** covered S&C were part of the Henry Ford Museum Collection, and the initials of HFM can be found on some pieces. Argus enjoyed a successful run from 1964-1973. This set is rather large and heavy. Colors available were crystal, medium blue, red and olive green.

have red-lids
olive
clear/lid
Blue/lid

No. 2770, Argus. Fostoria called this medium blue color: cobalt.

The beautifully shaped **No. 2834, Coventry** was sold only during 1970; in crystal and Honey Gold.

No. 2834, Coventry. Courtesy Brandon Dowd.

2700
Sugar
Height 2¾ in.

2700
Cream
Height 3¼ in.

No. 2700, Radiance.

No. 2700, Radiance is a short-lived dinnerware line from 1956-1957. The only known colors are crystal and yellow. Scarce in crystal, rare in yellow.

No. 2691, Decorator was in the catalogs from 1955-1957 and all parts of the 4-pc. set are rare. Crystal only.

2691

No. 2691, Decorator.

Fostoria	Crystal	Amber	Brown	Yellow	Green	Pink	Blue	Other
#2650 Horizon, sugar or creamer				$9	$12 (spruce)			
#2666 Contour, Individual sugar or creamer	$5 +							
#2666 Contour, large sugar or creamer	$5 +							
#2666 Contour, tray	$10 +							
#2685 Seascape, Individual sugar or creamer						$9	$10	
#2685 Seascape, large sugar or creamer						$16	$17	
#2685 Seascape, tray						$13	$15	
#2691 Decorator, any piece	trtp							
#2700 Radiance, sugar or creamer	$14			trtp				
#2718 Fairmont, sugar or creamer	trtp	$7			$12		$15	
#2719 Jamestown, sugar or creamer	$8	$10	$11		$14	$17	$17	$22 (amethyst)
#2770 Argus, sugar with lid	$15				$18 (olive)		$32	$24 (red)
#2770 Argus, creamer	$10				$13 (olive)		$25	$20 (red)
#2806 Pebble Beach, sugar with lid	trtp			$19		$38		$25 (smoke)
#2806 Pebble Beach, creamer	trtp			$12		$20		$15 (smoke)
#2834 Coventry, sugar or creamer	$7 *	$10 *						
#4186 Mesa, sugar with lid	$9	$9	$9		$9 (olive)		$21	
#4186 Mesa, creamer	$5	$5	$5		$5 (olive)		$12	

+ Simple metal adds 20% to price. Simple cuttings add 50%.
* Add 20% for simple crystal etching.

No. 2785, Gourmet was available from the mid-1960s until 1970 in crystal only. Pieces can be found with gold or platinum rims. The bases of this S&C look like a 6-sided cog or spoke.

Beginning in 1970 and continuing until the company closed it's doors, Fostoria sold new and reissued crystal S&C sets as part of their various giftware collections: No. 1704, Rosby, No. 2183 1/2, Colonial Prism, No. 2412, large Colony, No. 2574 large Raleigh, and No. 2710, Daisy & Button. The No. 2222 footed Individual creamer was mated with a newly made sugar and given the line name of **Virginia** (see page 45). All of these S&C sets found new life as crystal giftware items.

In addition, several completely new S&C were also introduced. No. **2377/677** & **686** (a variant of No. 2183, Colonial Prism from the 1920s), and No. **TR05/686, Transition** made brief appearances as the company was winding down.

In 1972-1973, Fostoria introduced another crystal giftware line which they called the *Heritage Collection*. The covered sugar and creamer known as **No. 682, Heritage** was part of this collection.

Unknown "diamond hobnail" creamer (which was sold with a handleless sugar as a set), found with Fostoria labels.

Fostoria	crystal
All crystal items from the giftware collections price from the $5 range (Colony, Raleigh) up to $16 for sugars with lids. Demand and collectability drops off sharply for items produced after 1970.	
Items with original labels will price 20% higher than those without.	

No. 2785, Gourmet.

2377/677

2377/686

have

No. 682, Heritage.

No. TR05/686, Transition. Round labels indicate the item was sold through the Fostoria Outlet store.

FRY

The Fry Glassware Company had a short but vibrant history making tableware between 1901 and 1933. Their colors are some of the most beautiful. You can find sugar and creamer sets in: Canary (vaseline), Rose (pink), Emerald (medium green), Azure (light blue), Royal (not quite cobalt), Crystal, Black (not amethyst), Golden Glow (amber) and Fuchsia (amethyst). Unfortunately, there isn't much information available on Fry, and exact dates are difficult to establish.

No. 802
Sugar and Cream

When you find Fry S&C with applied handles, look carefully for a heat-related stress crack at the top of the handle where it meets the glass. This is called a *heat check*, and several times I've seen where two cracks form a triangular shape only to have a chip result when the damage cracked all the way through. Some folks maintain that a heat check is still *mint condition* because the damage originated at the factory. You get to form your own opinion on that. I can't say why Fry handles tend toward this, but it may be due to how slender they are in comparison to handles from the other Elegant glass houses.

No 802 in Azure. Note the polished pontil mark.

No. 802 is a lookalike shape similar to shapes made by the other glass companies. It came with and without internal optics. Pieces with optics will have 20 internal panels which (so far) is a number I have found unique to Fry. The internal optic isn't always easy to see in a photo, so if you are making a purchase online, make sure you verify the number of panels.

Fry pieces have a smooth circle in the base which is known as a polished *pontil* mark. Both plain and optic pieces have this same mark in their bases. Sugars stand at just over 2 5/8" tall (at the rim) and they are noticeably shorter than the creamers. Creamers vary in height but they will generally measure at 3 3/8" to 3 1/2" to the top of their handle. On most of the lookalikes, the sugars and creamers are close to the same height. Fry handles are slender and delicate. The sugar handles generally do not extend in height above the rim.

No. 802 with heat check which cracked through.

No. 802 with no optic. Crystal with amethyst handles.

No. 802 black with elaborate silver overlay. Courtesy Carla Maningas.

No. 40007, Diamond Optic is known in crystal and the colors shown below.

No. 40007

No. 40007, Diamond Optic. Courtesy Kay & Dave Tucker.

Fry Collectors call the set below **Square Foot** as the Fry catalog number is unknown. Sets have been found in all the Fry colors.

Square Foot in black.

The name Square Foot is a bit misleading in that the base has eight points which alternate with eight scallops. The rim has the same point-scallop shape. This piece is frequently misidentified as LE Smith's Mt. Pleasant.

Crystal Square Foot with green stagecoach etching. White sugar used to highlight decoration.

No. 4007, crystal with black handles. Black sand used to highlight cutting.

No. 4007. Courtesy Kay & Dave Tucker. This black set has no internal optic panels while the green sample below has 20 internal panels.

No. 4007 came in all of the Fry colors as well as crystal with colored handles (previous page). S&C are found both with and without internal optics. There are two lookalikes which I've shown alongside a green No. 4007 below. The smaller amethyst sugar has a rough pontil mark and was made by Blenko. Blenko's amethyst looks both black and amethyst, depending on the light. In contrast, Fry's black looks black and Fry's amethyst looks amethyst. The Blenko set can also be found in red, which is not a color that Fry made. The crystal lookalike shown is an unknown. In comparison to No. 4007, the handles of the crystal piece are heavier at the bottom and the base is thicker.

Above from left to right: Unknown crystal with silver overlaid rim and handles, Fry No. 4007 with internal optics, and Blenko in amethyst.

The crystal pontil mark is polished smooth and the base around it has been ground flat. The Fry pontil is polished, but the base is not ground. The Blenko pontil mark is unpolished and has rough spots.

This is the No. 2000 shape. It is most often found in Foval glass (see next page). "Reeded" is the term for the treatment that you see going around the top of these pieces. This set also has a controlled bubble treatment. It's possible to find reeded pieces without the bubbles and bubbled pieces without the reeding. Other companies produced similar enhancements. Courtesy Kay & Dave Tucker.

Fry's **Foval** glass is a beautiful translucent pearl colored quality glass that has the added attraction of being heat-treated for durability. Durability is a good thing for glass approaching its 100th birthday.

The **No. 2000** blank is the Foval shape most easily found by today's collector. This S&C was sold as a standalone set and as part of at least seven different Tea Sets. S&C sets can be found with Pearl, Delft blue, or Jade green handles. Pearl handles are the least desirable. There is also a truly rare raspberry colored handle, but I was unable to acquire a photo. Delft and Jade trims are equally scarce, regardless of the fact that I was unable to locate a photo of the Jade colored handles.

Sets can be found plain, with a *stipple* treatment or with the *Festoon* treatment. Festoon consisted of colored glass fused to the Pearl glass in a looping pattern. Festoon can be found in both Delft and Jade trim.

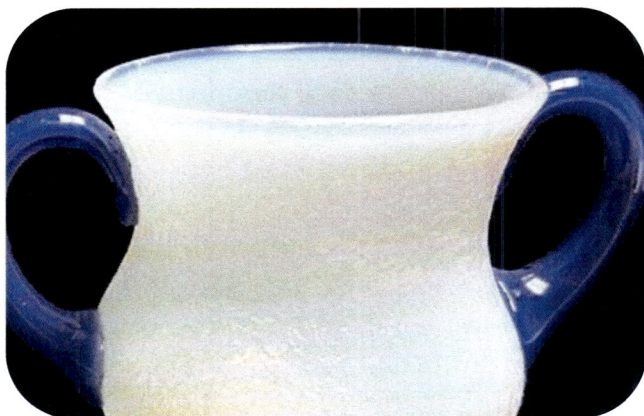

Foval with Festoon treatment.
Courtesy Judy Kaufman. Photographer Mike Sabo.

No. 2000 with silver decoration by the Rockwell Silver Company.
Courtesy Kay & Dave Tucker.

No. 2000 with Delft blue handles and stipple treatment,
above and below. Courtesy Dave Lippert.

There are other Foval S&C shapes which appear on occasion, but with much less frequency than No. 2000. No. 2001 is known with both Delft and Jade handles but the set did not come with a pearl colored handle.

No. 2001, Foval. Courtesy John Zastowney.

A third bulbous-shaped Foval set appears very infrequently and is shown below in silhouette. I have only seen the bulbous shape with the Jade trim but Delft is certainly possible. The line number is unknown.

The shape below I found in a Fry catalog, of which I was only able to view a poor quality microfiche copy. Much of the detail was missing but It was a distinctive shape, so I filled in the outline so you could get an idea of this very unusual blank. There was no date on the catalog, but the Nos. 2000 and 2001 sugar and creamer were also shown. The set was identified as **No. 811, Foval**.

A fifth Foval shape appears below and it may be a one of a kind set. No line number is known.

Foval S&C with unique blue trimmed rim and foot. Courtesy Judy Kaufman. Photographer Mike Sabo.

Fry also produced a number of sugar and creamer sets in crystal which are considered to be part of the American Brilliant Cut Glass period. These pieces are not part of this collectible guide as they are a different genre.

Fry Sugar or Creamer	
#802, amber, crystal with colored handles	$20
#802, pink, green	$30-$45
#802, any other color	$50-$75
#4007, crystal with black handles	$20 +
#4007, amethyst, black	$20-$25 +
#4007, green, cobalt	$25-$30 +
#40007, any color	trtp
Foval, #2000, pearl handles	$35
Foval, #2000, colored handles	$45 ++ / +++
Foval, #2001, colored handles	$75-$90
Foval, Shape #3, colored handles	$60-$75
Foval, any other shape	trtp
Square Foot, amber	$10
Square Foot, any other color	$15-$18

+ Decorated pieces with simple metal bands add 50%. Cuttings 2x plain.
++ Rockwell decoration is trtp. Stippling and Festoon are trtp.
+++ Raspberry handles are trtp

The Pairpoint Glass company made pieces in a Foval-like translucent glass with crystal handles. These pieces are often mistaken for Fry. The shape of the Pairpoint sugar and creamer is distinctly Pairpoint, so if you pay attention to the shapes, you won't be misled.

Pairpoint sugar and creamer. Courtesy Dave Lippert.

Look for the 𝐇 *Monogram*

HAZEL-ATLAS GLASS COMPANY - Wheeling, W. Va.

1924 advertisement.

Early in the 20th Century, the bottle making companies of Hazel and Atlas merged and became the Hazel-Atlas Glass Company. Utilitarian items such as bottles, jars and tumblers were their primary focus until the mid-1920s when they began to market crystal tableware items. Green closely followed crystal and by the mid-1930s, whole dinnerware sets were being produced in crystal, green, cobalt, amethyst, pink, yellow, black and what was to become a huge seller for H-A, the durable, opaque white glass known as **Platonite**.

Colonial. Courtesy Karen Plott.

There were two early crystal sugar and creamer sets which began appearing in mail order catalogs in the mid-1920s. The sugar lids of both sets had a stubby, hard to grasp finial and the creamer spout was pulled down from the rim. Advertising indicates that the name **Colonial** was used for both sets for a time, even though one was a block design and the other had plain vertical panels. The set with the vertical panels continues to be known as Colonial.

There is some dispute amongst researchers about the proper line name for the blocked S&C which eventually became part of a larger dinnerware line. The Butler Brothers catalog in 1927 used the name **Colonial Block** and the Sears catalog (reprint below) used the word Colonial. Colonial Block is the most commonly used name by collectors.

Six-Piece Colonial Table Set
Covered butter dish (2 pieces), covered sugar bowl (2 pieces), one spoonholder and one cream pitcher. Pressed glass.

Weight, packed, 12 pounds.
35L6805—Per set.................**$1.15**

A mid-1920s Sears catalog reprint showing the stubby finial on both the sugar and butter lids.

A recently uncovered 1930s company catalog used the line name of **Modernistic** for the block patterned tableware. Unfortunately, during the same period company advertising used the word *modernistic* as a pronoun in describing the tableware. So it appears that the company didn't know what to call the block patterned line and use of the term modernistic was somewhat fluid. It seems as if someone in the company really liked the word because it was used in future advertising even after the block patterned tableware was discontinued in the mid-1930s.

I use the name Colonial Block because it is the most well known and appears to be one of the oldest known names used for the line

Colonial, from company catalog after the finial change.

In the late 1920s, advertisements show that the stubby finial on the lid was replaced with an easier to grasp knob finial. By 1930, the company had introduced both Colonial Block and Colonial in green. Green Colonial Block is readily found but green Colonial pieces are scarce.

At some point after 1930, the creamer spout was redesigned to include extra glass above the rim. Pink appears to have been introduced after the creamer spout was changed; as all pink creamers have the new spout. Ironically, most green creamers found today have the old style spout and the newer built-up green creamers are much harder to locate.

White Colonial Block was made in the 1950s as part of a milk glass promotion known as *Early American Opaque.*

Colonial Block with built-up creamer spout.

Cobalt creamers can be found both with and without the Shirley Temple decal. Those creamers with the decal have a flat, non-blocked surface which frames the white graphic. At least one cobalt creamer without the flattened space and decal is known. Sadly, there is no known matching cobalt sugar for either style of creamer. Both styles of cobalt creamer are rare.

Cobalt creamer with Shirley Temple decal.
Courtesy Jean & Vic Laermans.

Powder jars are found with Hazel-Atlas-styled lids on what appears to be a Hocking **Block Optic** sherbet base. It is unknown if these lidded jars were made by Hazel-Atlas. It is not possible to marry a powder lid with an actual sugar base as the black lids are too small.

X-Design with older spout pulled down from the rim.

X-Design (collector's name) was probably introduced around the same time that Colonial Block came out in green as no crystal X-Design sugar or creamer is known to exist. X-Design is only found with the knob finial, but you can find creamers with both the pulled down spout and the built-up spout. The two different styles of creamer have two different Hazel-Atlas logos. One has the logo inside a circle, the other has no circle.

Crisscross was a line of kitchenware and utility dishes to which Hazel-Atlas added the sugar and creamer. Crisscross sets are easily found in crystal, scarce in green and rare in pink. A collector once told me that he had heard about a cobalt blue set. This seems likely but I haven't been able to confirm the rumor.

Crisscross, courtesy Key & Dave Tucker.

New Century was introduced in the early 1930s. The sugar (No. 1789), lid (No. 1789 1/2), and creamer (No. 1788) were sold in green and crystal. Crystal pieces, especially the lids, are elusive to locate but even when found, they don't generate much interest with collectors.

| 1788   Cream | 1789 Sugar and 1789½ Cover |

New Century as shown in an early colored catalog from the 1930s.

Starlight is a little appreciated tableware line which came in crystal and Platonite. The sugar and creamer from this line has so far only appeared in crystal. Collectors virtually ignore this S&C. Production was for a short window in the late 1930s.

Starlight.

Ribbon (collector's name), courtesy Dave Lippert.

	crystal	white	green	pink
Colonial, sugar with lid *	$7		$40	
Colonial, creamer	$5		$10	
Colonial Block, sugar with early lid	$14 +		trtp	
Colonial Block, sugar with later lid	$10 +	$17	$22	$40
Colonial Block, creamer **	$7 +	$12	$14	$20
Crisscross, sugar with lid	$10		$130	$160
Crisscross, creamer	$7		$60	$75
New Century, sugar with lid	$16		$22	
New Century, creamer	$9		$14	
Starlight, sugar or creamer	<$5			
X-Design, sugar with lid			$24	
X-Design, creamer			$17	
* Early and later Colonial lids sell for the same price				
** Cobalt creamers are trtp				
+ Add 50% for pieces found with star cuttings in the blocks.				

Cloverleaf, black with unusual gold trim. Courtesy Karen Plott.

Ribbon, Ovide and **Cloverleaf** may have been the earliest sugar and creamer sets which Hazel-Atlas made, even before Colonial. These three very similar S&C were sold as standalone sets through mail-order catalogs in the mid-1920s. These catalogs do not have any names assigned but only describe the pieces as *Sugars, Creamers and Sets.* Later, all three S&C pairs initially became part of small tableware lines. As the 1930s progressed, Ovide got new handles and a opaque retrofit, Cloverleaf became part of a large, successful dinnerware line, and Ribbon faded away.

There is no known documentation indicating that the name *Ovide* was used by Hazel-Atlas. At this point in time it is assumed to be a collector's name. For the purpose of this publication, the earliest, pre-opaque, Ovide will be called **Old Ovide**.

Old Ovide crystal with cutting.

The Cloverleaf S&C came in green, black and yellow. Note how the ad at right illustrates the green creamer with a spout which is pulled down from the rim, while the black (previous page) and yellow (below) creamer spouts are built above the rim. Green creamers are found with both styles of spout. No other color was made with a pulled down spout. This indicates that green production predated both yellow and black for a time.

Yellow Cloverleaf.

Around 1933, the **Ovide** S&C got a new handle with a notch for the consumer's thumb and a heat resistant white body. Colors were fired-on over the white glass. That heat resistant white glass was called *Platonite*. No notch handled Ovide has been found in transparent glass, so the design break appears to be clean.

GREEN GLASSWARE
Matched Pieces To Retail at 5c . . . 10c and 15c

PROCESS ETCHED BORDER! Transparent pressed glass . . . good quality . . . . THIN edges . . . with a brilliant sheen finish. The NEW CLOVER LEAF BORDER gives this line immediate sales appeal. ORDER NOW—START SELLING!

A. SALAD PLATES
CO-1091 — 8 in. diameter.
3 doz. in carton, 33 lbs.
Doz 82c

B. CREAMERS
CO-1093 — 3¾ in. high.
3 doz. in carton, 24 lbs.
Doz 65c

C. SUGAR BOWLS
CO-1094 — 3¾ in. high.
3 doz. in carton, 24 lbs.
Doz 65c

D. FOOTED TUMBLERS
CO-1100 — 9½ in., 5¾ in. high. 6 doz. in carton, 40 lbs.
Doz 48c

E. COVD. CANDY JARS
CO-1101 — 6¼ in. high.
3 doz. in carton, 40 lbs.
Doz $1.05

F. FOOTED SHERBETS
CO-1099 — 5 oz., 3⅛ in. high. 6 doz. in carton, 25 lbs.
Doz 36c

G. SHERBET PLATES
CO-1092 — 6 in. diameter.
3 doz. in carton, 20 lbs.
Doz 40c

H. CUPS & SAUCERS
CO-1090 — Cup 3⅛x2¼ in., saucer 5½ in. (Our price includes cup & saucer—24 pieces to the dozen). 3 doz. in carton, 35 lbs.
Doz 92c

J. SALTS & PEPPERS
CO-1102 — 3¾ in. high.
4 doz. in carton, 12 lbs.
Doz 54c

K. NAPPIES
CO-1096 — 4 in. diameter. deep shape. 6 doz. in carton, 35 lbs.
Doz 30c

N. GRILL PLATES
CO-1095 — 10¼ in. diameter, 3 compartments. 2 doz. in carton, 50 lbs.
Doz $1.50

L. CEREAL DISHES
CO-1097 — 5 in. diameter. extra deep. 4 doz. in carton, 36 lbs.
Doz 60c

M. BERRY BOWLS
CO-1098 — 7 in. diameter. extra deep. 3 doz. in carton, 50 lbs.
Doz 92c

1931 Butler Brothers catalog.

From left to right: Ovide, Old Ovide and LE Smith's No. 1903. Ovide is Platonite underneath a fired-on black exterior. The center and right sugars are both black glass. Comparing the necks above each base readily illustrates the noticeably thicker Ovide shape.

The thumb-notch handle of Ovide is distinctive enough that you shouldn't mistake it for anything else. But, identification can be trickier between Old Ovide and the Smith pieces. Smith handles are thicker, the bowl is taller, and the ring above the base is slightly thinner. But, unless you are making a side by side comparison, these subtle differences may not jump out at you. The differences between the Old Ovide and Smith creamers are even less noticeable than those on the sugars.

If you are faced with making a determination between Old Ovide and Smith and can't readily tell them apart, turn the pieces over and look at the well in the base. The Smith indentation is a clearly defined round circle. The Old Ovide well is a sloping indentation. Both companies made crystal, black, and transparent green S&C. LE Smith is also known to have made a transparent pink.

Above and below: LE Smith No. 1903 (left) and Old Ovide (right) showing the differences in the bases.

Old Ovide with yellow floral etching. White sugar used for design clarification. Courtesy Karen Plott.

Old Ovide with unusual gold trimmed decal decoration. Courtesy Karen Plott.

Old Ovide with alternating red and gold stripes. The gold looks black on the inside of the piece. Courtesy Glynis McCain.

"Floral Sterling" (collector's name) on Old Ovide blank. The silver decoration is frequently found in a faded condition. Beware, flash photography can make the flowers appear brighter than they really are. Bright, mint condition flowers are rare.

Old Ovide with unknown etching. Courtesy Lyle Fokken.

When I started working on this book, I was told there were 50 different Platonite-Ovide decorations which could be found. I doubted the story at first. But, as you will see on the following pages, there are more than 50 different decorations which I have documented. Some of these decorations have names, most are just a description. Have you seen any I have missed? About 25% of the Ovides you find will say *Hazel-Atlas* on the rim and about 5% will say *Platonite* in the well. This has no bearing on price.

3-Salmon with white interior and gold rim. 4-Flamingo. Courtesy Karen Plott.

1-White, 2-Pastel Pink. Courtesy Karen Plott.
Note: Whites can be found with varying levels of transparency.

5-Rust. Rust is common, but any color with painted flowers is very unusual. Courtesy Karen Plott.

6-Black.

14-Green with white interior. Courtesy Glynis McCain.

7-Teal, 8-Aqua, 9-Turquoise with white interior and gold rim.
Courtesy Karen Plott.

15-Chatreuse with green shading. Courtesy Karen Plott.

10, 11-Red and Orange with white interior. Courtesy Karen Plott.

*16, 17, 18-**Informal** in Pink, Blue and Yellow. Courtesy Karen Plott.*

12-Chartreuse, 13-Yellow with white interior next to a common
household item for color comparison. Courtesy Karen Plott.

*19-**Sunrise** (can be found with various intensities of shading) next to*
#13 for color comparison. Courtesy Karen Plott.

*20, 21-**Tulip** in red and blue. Courtesy Karen Plott.*

28-Gold, black, red, red, black stripes. Courtesy Karen Plott.

*22, 23-**Forget-Me-Not** in blue and red.*
Courtesy Karen Plott (blue) and Glynis McCain (red).

*29-Red **Arrowheads**, 30-Red band w/ 2 gold hairline stripes.*
Courtesy Karen Plott.

*24, 25-**Vine Flower** in red and blue. Courtesy Karen Plott.*

*31-**Diamonds & Dots**, 32-**Red Urn**. Courtesy Glynis McCain.*

*26-Red **Sweetheart**, 27-Red **Birds**. Courtesy Karen Plott.*
Note: Although not known, both 26 & 27 may also come in blue.

33-Red band w/ gold stripe inside, 34-Red band w/ small crest.
Courtesy Karen Plott.

*35-**Polka Dots**. Courtesy Glynis McCain.*

*41-Red, gold, red stripes w/ gold wreath, 42-**Tube Socks**.*

36-Black stripe, 37-Yellow stripe. Courtesy Doug Block.

*43-**Bouquet**, 44-**Black Floral**. Courtesy Karen Plott.*

*38-**Flying Geese**. Courtesy Jean & Vic Laermans.*

*45-Green diagonal stripes, 46-**Black Arbor**. Courtesy Karen Plott.*

39-Extra wide red band. Courtesy Chad Kirkland.
40-Extra wide blue band. Courtesy Glynis McCain.

47-Two red w/ three gold hairlines, 48-Red, black hairlines.
Courtesy Karen Plott.

*49--Blue w/ black stripes, 50-Green **Navajo.***

*55-**Windmill**. Courtesy Dick Ladd.*

*51-Black **Squiggle**, 52-Gold **Squiggle**. Courtesy Karen Plott.*

56-Pastel pink with decal.

53-White with single red stripe (white interior). Courtesy Karen Plott.

*57-**Art Deco**. Courtesy Kay & Dave Tucker.*

54-White with single red stripe (red interior). Courtesy Karen Plott.

White with black = Hazel-Atlas Squiggle.
Black with white = LE Smith Confetti decoration.

1938 Butler Brothers catalog.
Notice the dinnerware is called "Platonite", not Ovide.

Royal Lace advertising from the 1930s. Notice how cobalt is
represented in this early color photograph.

Sugar or Creamer	crystal	green	yellow	black
Cloverleaf		$11	$9	$8 *
Floral Sterling				$5 **
Old Ovide	$5 ***	$9		$12
Ribbon		$18		

* 3x for gold decoration
** Price shown is for typical, faded silver.
*** add 50% for simple cuttings, 2x for silver bands, 3x for colored bands and decals, sets with etchings are trtp.

Ovide Platonite Sugar or Creamer

Chartreuse, Rust, White **	>$5
Black, Flamingo, pastel pink	$7
Pastel aqua, teal	$16
Informal, any color	$6
Chartreuse w/ green shading, Sunrise	$7
Orange or yellow w/ white interior	$10
Green or red w/ white interior	$18
Salmon or Turquoise w/ white interior	$18 *
Arrowheads, Birds	$8 red / $25 blue
Black Floral, Bouquet	$10
Forget-Me-Not, Tulips, Vine Flower	$12 red / $18 blue
Squiggle, black or gold	$13
Stripes, red, any combination not specified	$6-$12
Black or yellow single stripe	$15
Stripes, blue or green	$15
Decals, floral	$15+
Sweetheart	$15
Extra Wide band	$17 red / $22 blue
Black Arbor, Navajo	$20
Hand painted, any color	$20+
Art Deco, Windmills, Flying Geese	trtp
Polka Dots, Diamonds Dots, Urn	trtp
White w/ red interior	trtp

* gold rims + 50%
** Chartreuse was sold in multi-colored sets called *Sierra*. Rust was sold in multi-colored sets called *Tempo*.
+ Values can range depending on the desirability of the design and the motivation of the buyer for a possible one-of-a-kind item.

Royal Lace was a dinnerware line which ran from the mid-30s into the early 1940s. The sugar and creamer sets were sold with and without the lid, which explains the frequent appearance of sugars without a lid. Royal Lace was available in cobalt blue, green, pink and crystal. The cobalt lid is particularly desirable and prices for it have remained strong.

1938 Butler Brothers catalog sold the sugar without the lid.

Royal Lace.

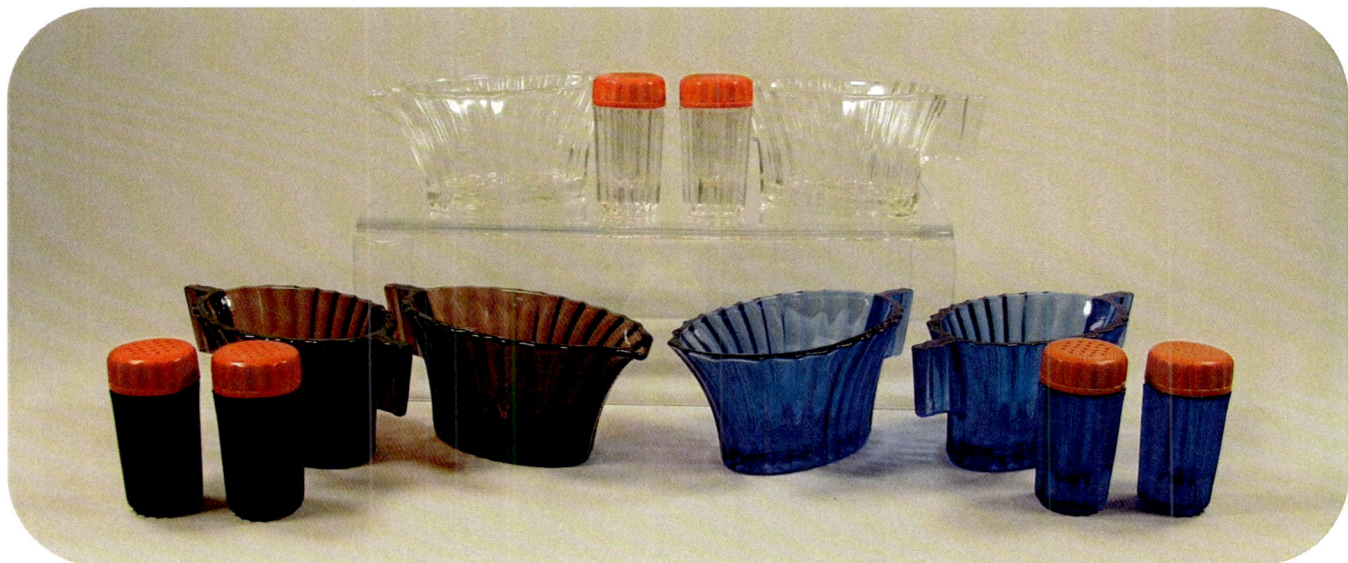

Standing Rib with matching shakers in crystal, amethyst, and cobalt. Courtesy Dennis Headrick.

The little ribbed sets above came in crystal, cobalt and amethyst. Once in a while you find a crystal set on a metal tray with the two shakers shown. While there is no known documentation giving us a name or a line number for this ribbed set, similar unidentified ribbed H-A pieces are known by the collectors name, ***Standing Rib***, so it seems reasonable to let this set become part of that group. This set is frequently mistaken for Heisey's individual *Ridgeleigh* sugar and creamer.

It is unknown exactly when the **Chevron** sugar and creamer was introduced. This set is found only in cobalt and pink. Hazel-Atlas may have sold the cobalt sugar and creamer in a 3-piece set with the slightly larger milk pitcher; as the three pieces appear together frequently. I am unaware of any pink milk pitchers being known at this time, but crystal milk pitchers can be found. You can easily find the cobalt S&C and while less available, pink is easy to find as well.

Chevron. Courtesy Karen Plott.

Florentine 1 ruffled S&C. Courtesy Darlene Shoppert.

Florentine is one dinnerware line which has been divided into two collectible subsets. Collectors call the hexagonal pieces **Florentine 1** and the round pieces **Florentine 2.** Both the S&C sets are round, but Collectors have assigned the S&C sets based on the dinnerware pieces they were most frequently shown/sold with in company catalogs and advertising.

There are two variations of the Florentine 1 S&C. A flat rim set (which came with a lid) and a ruffled rim set. Flat rim sets can be found in crystal, yellow, green, and pink.

Flat rim Florentine 1 5-pc set showing sugar with metal lid. Courtesy Darlene Shoppert.

Lids can easily acquire edge damage, so check carefully before paying full price. Pink lids are the most difficult to find.

Ruffled rims are found in crystal, pink, green, and cobalt. The most difficult ruffled rim set to find is green, but all of the colors have disappeared into private collections and are becoming harder to find.

Florentine 1 sugar and creamer sold as part of a 36-piece hexagonal dinner set in the 1933 Butler Brothers catalog.

Note the nearly flat rim on the sugar. The most desirable sets have a distinct flared ruffle. This is the only Florentine set that came in cobalt.

Florentine 1 with rare metallic overlay. Possibly a one-of-a-kind set. Courtesy Kay & Dave Tucker.

It appears from the catalogs and advertisements I've been able to view that both the Florentine 1 & 2 sugars were always sold with a lid. Lids and sugar bowls have stuck together over the decades and most sugars are found with their lid today. Even the chrome metal lid shows up on a semi-regular basis, though it is often found on some random bowl instead of being mated to the Florentine 1 sugar. The one notable exception to this is the crystal Florentine 2 lid. Only a few are known to exist.

Once in a while you will find Florentine 2 S&C with a fired-on color over crystal. Known colors are red, light blue, light yellow and teal. These sets are never found with a lid.

You can find a Florentine 2, yellow, round condiment tray which holds the S&C and a set of tall shakers. These trays came only in yellow and putting together a condiment set may be pricey, but it's worth it to have this gem in your collection.

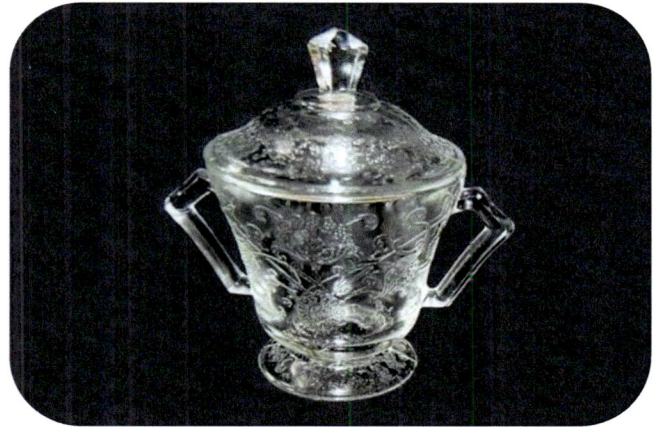

Rare Florentine 2 lid in crystal. Courtesy Dick Ladd.

	Crystal	Pink	Cobalt	Green	Amethyst
Chevron		$10	$6		
Royal Lace, creamer	$10	$12	$19	$11	
Royal Lace, sugar w/lid	$14	$30	$90	$40	
Standing Rib	$5		$12		$8

Florentine 1 & 2	Crystal	Yellow	Pink	Green
1 - Sugar w/ lid, flat rim	$12	$15	$18	$24
1 - Sugar with metal lid	$15			
1 - Creamer, flat rim	$8	$10	$12	$14
1 - Sugar or creamer, ruffled rim	$11		$24	$100
2 - Sugar w/lid	$26	$14		$19
2 - Creamer	$5 +	$10		$14
2 - Condiment set, 6 piece set		$140		
1 - Cobalt ruffled, each piece	$40			

+ Crystal with silver or gold rim add 20%, with painted rim 2x plain crystal
* Fired-on colors over crystal $12 (yellow), $17– $20 (all others)

Florentine 2 with shakers and condiment tray. Courtesy Dick Ladd.

Teal fired-on color. Courtesy Darlene Sheppert.

Light blue fired-on color.

Newport in amethyst with unusual silver overlay.

The **Newport** S&C (aka Hairpin) were first introduced in the mid-1930s in cobalt and amethyst. Newport tableware was made in crystal and pink but no S&C are known in those two colors.

The Platonite white sets with fired-on colors were introduced in the late 1930s alongside other H-A Platonite dinnerware lines. The solid white sets may have been sold into the 1940s. Fired-on colors include: yellow, orange, teal, pink and light blue. Other colors may have been made.

Newport dessert sets were sold which contained a dark green sugar and a Chartreuse yellow creamer. This set is frequently found intact today. I have not seen a dark green creamer or a Chartreuse sugar, which may explain why these bi-colored sets have remained intact.

The breakfast sets on metal trays (shown above) were advertised in a retail catalog in cobalt but may have also been sold in amethyst. Notice the contraption on the back of the tray in the illustration directly above. That is a toast holder.

It is unknown if Hazel-Atlas put these sets together or if it was the work of an outside company.

Newport fired-on yellow over Platonite.

Close-up of red plastic finial.

"TRUE BLUE" GLASS

In The Lovely Moderntone Design!

Moderntone was introduced in the mid-1930s in transparent amethyst, cobalt, pink, crystal and plain white Platonite. Crystal isn't found very often, but no one seems to care. Pink is rare. Cobalt pieces can be found with both gold and silver rims.

The colored pieces with white interiors were introduced in the late 1930s; and by 1940 the interiors were colored. The blanks for these pieces were Platonite. Various decorations and colors continued in the Hazel-Atlas catalogs until the 1950s. Pieces with a white interior are generally harder to find than the solid colored pieces, and prices are just starting to reflect this as the white interior pieces disappear into private collections.

Cobalt, crystal and amethyst Moderntone. Courtesy Karen Plott.

*The fitted metal lid (above) seems to be the most available lid for the Moderntone sugar. During the Depression era, sugar lids typically did not have a spoon notch, but mayonnaise lids did. Perhaps this is because granulated sugar was a novelty in the early part of the century; and most sugar was either cubed or served in chunks with tongs. The bowl with the red finial lid may have been marketed as a condiment dish. Not shown is a loose-fitting, third style of lid which has a black plastic finial. Above photo courtesy Jean & Vic Laermans.
Below photo courtesy Dick Ladd.*

Pink Moderntone. Courtesy Jean & Vic Laermans.

Four stripes. Courtesy Glynis McCain.

White Moderntone can be found in plain white with some translucence, opaque white, and white with blue, red, green, black or gold stripes. The more stripes, the more desirable the decoration is. The red Willow decoration shown below is found in blue on plates, so blue might also exist on the S&C.

Moderntone with red Willow decoration.
Courtesy Jean & Vic Laermans.

Single color and multiple color sets were available in 15, 32 and 44-piece combinations. One specific set included a pastel green sugar and a pastel yellow creamer. This same pair is commonly found together today. If you don't like mismatched sugars and creamers, there is both a pastel green creamer and a pastel yellow sugar which can be purchased.

The catalog snippets shown at right (from top to bottom) indicate the progression of Moderntone from plain white in 1934, to white interiors in 1938, and finally the solid one-color pieces in 1940. The 1938 catalog ad on the previous page gives us an idea of when the term *Moderntone* may have come into use. It appears that at least for a time, the company may have preferred the name *Carnival* for the opaque colored dishes.

"CARNIVAL" GLASS TABLEWARE
shades to retail at popular prices. Carry all colors—green, orange and yellow—

4¾ In. Handled Cream Soups—3 doz in ctn. 21 lbs. 5OR-1354—Green } Doz 5OR-1404—Orange } T. O. 5OR-1424—Yellow } Less quantity. Doz	Sugar Bowls and Cream Pitchers—3½ in. high, asstd. evenly. 3 doz in ctn, 19 lbs. 5OR-1358—Green } 5OR-1408—Orange } Doz T. O. 5OR-1428—Yellow } Less quantity. Doz

No. 0-628G—15 piece set; Green glass; 5 plates, 4 cups, 4 saucers, 1 sugar bowl and 1 creamer. Weight per set, 12
No. 0-628R—Red Glass, otherwise same as No. 0-628G.
No. 0-628Y—Yellow Glass, otherwise same as No. 0-628G.
Per set $2.50

It's purely a novelty to note that the 1953 Butler Brothers catalog sold a set of Ovide with a tag line which read, *Sugar and creamer in chartreuse. All other colors evenly assorted in new moderntone colors: burgundy, forest green, and chartreuse, and burgundy and green* (in later catalogs gray dishes were added to these colors.) The word "moderntone" was not capitalized in the description but these sets can be found complete in boxes with the words "Moderntone Tableware" emblazoned in large letters on the side. As in the case of Colonial Block aka Modernistic, the company clearly was flexible with the use of certain line names making research using written records alone difficult.

Crystal Hobnail atop an original box. The pieces were found in this box but the source of the decoration is unknown. Courtesy Karen Plott.

In the 1960s, **Hobnail** was the name for a crystal set with a hobnail base. The same set was later introduced in turquoise blue and the name was changed to **Capri**.

As with other line names, Hazel-Atlas was inconsistent with their branding. Capri is the line name of the turquoise S&C with the hobnail base, it is also the line name for a similar turquoise set with a large twist pattern in the bowl. Collectors call this blank: *Capri Swirl.*

Capri Hobnail is uncommon but Capri Swirl is rare.

All Ripple photos courtesy Karen Plott.

In 1957, Hazel-Atlas was purchased by the Continental Can Company and their tableware began to display the brand name of *Hazelware*.

Ripple (aka *Crinoline*) was introduced after the 1957 name change. All Ripple S&C are white; and the aqua or pink colors are fired on over the white base. Handles were made in both the beaded and plain styles but for today's collector, the beaded handle is the most desirable. Some creamers have pulled down spouts from the rim and others have the built-up spout shown on the pink set above.

Capri creamer with original label. Courtesy Jean & Vic Laermans.

Do you ever wonder about these little cubed pieces? Hazel-Atlas or Jeannette? They are both, actually. The crystal sugar on the left is Jeannette and the pink sugar on the right is Hazel-Atlas. So, how do you tell? Look at the rims, Jeannette has a sharper point. Now look at the first row of blocks which reflect as a flattened diamond shape, the Jeannette pattern makes a larger diamond. **Cubist** is a popular collector name for these pieces and there are clues which point out that Cubist may have been the official name for one of these sets.

White set with original labels (above). Amber sugar (below). Amber S&C are found in boxes marked "Hazelware". Courtesy Karen Plott.

Jeannette base on left with a wider ring, Hazel-Atlas base on right.

Notice the bottoms of the sugars above. Both pieces have a ring around the circumference of the base. The Jeannette ring is wider.

Jeannette pieces were sold as part of a 3-piece set with a tray in plain crystal, crystal with a gold rim, and satinized pastel colors. Stained red sets were Jeannette blanks sold by Pilgrim Glass.

There are a ton of these little S&C sets available today, but you will find five Hazel-Atlas sets for every Jeannette set you locate.

Some H-A sets have a small button in the middle of their rays. The milk glass pieces have the HA logo on their button. The pink pieces do not have a button and you can find crystal Hazel-Atlas sets with and without this button. The pink pieces may have been made as early as the 1930s when Hazel-Atlas was making other pink glass items. Pieces found with the button can be dated to the 1950s and 60s.

The confusion surrounding the cube-shaped lookalikes just keeps getting better. There are two pink imitators floating around, possibly in your local antique mall.

Unknown pink cube lookalikes.

The left example has a rounded handle which is flat at the top with a little knob on it's shoulders. The rim has the typical points and the base has a lookalike pedestal foot. The right example has a flat base (no pedestal) and a completely flat rim. I have not figured out who made either of these little pink lookalike sets as of yet.

Then we have Fostoria American. There really is no good reason to confuse American with any of the cube lookalikes. American has a rounded handle which looks nothing like any of the other handles. In addition, American has a quality, and a polished sparkle that none of the lookalikes have. It's not that folks call the crystal Fostoria pieces, *Hazel-Atlas* or *Jeannette*, it's always the other way around. I can not count the times I have seen pink Hazel-Atlas cubed S&C advertised as rare pink American. There actually is a rare pink American S&C set which sits on a rare pink tray. More photos of Fostoria American pieces are located in the Fostoria chapter and on the front cover of this book.

Fostoria American (left), Hazel-Atlas (right).

5½ OZ. CUBIST CREAMER	6½ OZ. CUBIST SUGAR
Pressed and Blown Tableware; Packed in 6 doz. cartons; Average weight 28 lbs.	Pressed and Blown Tableware; Packed in 6 doz. cartons; Average weight 33 lbs.
No. U-1251 . . . . Per 100 17.50	No. U-1250 . . . . Per 100 17.90

The above illustration is from a Marshall-Wells catalog with a circa 1950s date. While it's not absolute that Hazel-Atlas supplied the sugar and creamer that this company sold, the nearly flat rim and flattened diamonds indicate Hazel-Atlas as the manufacturer. In addition, this set was sold alongside another Hazel-Atlas S&C set, No. 326/327 (see next page). Note the name assigned to the little S&C...Cubist. Jeannette catalogs from the 1960s listed their set as No. 600, with no name. It's not proof by any means, but I suspect Hazel-Atlas may have called their set "Cubist" and that name has stuck around creating confusion and controversy to this day.

Beehive (collector's name).

Beehive is a line about which almost nothing is known. The Platonite S&C are shown in company catalogs from the 1950s, but I've not been able to find a reference for either the crystal or pink sets. My guess is the pink pieces were made in the late 1930s when the company was making other pink glass items. Crystal was probably made at the same time and may have continued into the 1940s.

Pink sets are the most difficult to find and you'll locate ten crystal sets for every pink set you see.

No. 326 creamer, No. 327 1/2 sugar with lid, and No. 327 sugar.

Shown in mail order catalogs from the early 1950s through the 1961 Hazelware catalog is the **No. 326/327** sugar and creamer set. A similar set was made by the Libbey Glassware company in the 1970s. Shown below is a Hazel-Atlas sugar next to a Libby creamer. Note how the H-A piece flares out slightly at the bottom while the Libbey piece is straight .

No. 327 1/2 sugar (left), Libbey No. 5095 (right). Courtesy Karen Plott.

Satinized Nos. 326 creamer and 327 sugar with silver overlay. Courtesy Susan Spirk.

Libbey Glass Nos. 5095 creamer and 5096 sugar.

Newport	sugar or creamer
Amethyst, transparent	$14 *
Cobalt, transparent	$12 *
Fired on colors, white interior	$7-$10
Fired on colors, colored interior	$6
White	$8
* 2x for sugars with metal lid, 3x for silver overlay	

Moderntone (exterior / interior)	sugar or creamer
Crystal	$6
Amethyst, transparent	$8
Pink, transparent	trtp
Burgundy, rust, white	<$5
Cobalt, transparent	$5 +
Pastel green/green sugar	<$5 (sugar only)
Pastel yellow/yellow creamer	<$5 (creamer only)
Pastel yellow/white, pink/pink	$7
Pink/white	$10
Orange/white, Bright yellow/white	$8
Pastel blue/blue	$10
Pastel green/white	$10
Pastel blue/white	$14
Pastel green/green creamer	$15 (creamer only)
Pastel yellow/yellow sugar	$15 (sugar only)
Teal green/teal green	$15
Royal blue/white	$18
Teal green/white	$20
White/one stripe, red, gold or black	$6
White/one stripe, green or blue	$10
White/two stripes, red	$10
White/two stripes, blue	$14
White/four or five stripes, red	$18
White/four or five stripes, black or blue	$25
White/red Willow decals	$32
Lid, metal finial	$30
Lid, red finial	$35
Lid, black finial	$45
+ add 50% for mint condition metal decorations.	

Hazel-Atlas	crystal	white	pink	aqua
Beehive, creamer	$5	$12	$15	
Beehive, sugar w/lid	$7	$16	$22	
Capri, Hobnail creamer				$16
Capri, Hobnail sugar w/lid				$24
Capri, Swirl				trtp
Cubist	<$5	$7 (amber also)	$10	
Hobnail, creamer	$8 *			
Hobnail, sugar w/ lid	$15 *			
No. 326/327	<$5 *			
No 327 1/2 w/ lid	$6			
Ripple, plain handle		$8	$15	$18
Ripple, beaded handle		$10 *	$17	$21
* 2x for painted decorations, 3x for silver & satin				

Heisey began producing glass in 1896. During their first twenty years they produced an extraordinary number of different sugars and creamers. The company ceased glass making in 1957, and in 1958 all the remaining assets, including the molds, were transferred to the Imperial Glass Company. Heisey gave today's collector nearly 200 different S&C blanks. This Elegant glass was well made and it's not uncommon to find 100-year-old pieces in near mint condition. Most of the earliest S&C sets are highly sought after and finding them can be difficult and expensive.

There was no ideal way to list dates in this chapter. The dates shown generally reflect when the overall line was in the catalogs, not the exact dates for when the set was produced. Please note that the rare nature of some sets would indicate that they were not made for the full span of the dates listed. If researchers disagreed about exact production years, I generalized the information. As with all the data presented here, it is a first step to more in-depth knowledge and there are many resources available if you are interested in knowing a more exact production date for any Heisey S&C.

No. 1200, Cut Block Table S&C with spooner. 1896-1903. Cut Block was the first sugar and creamer produced by Heisey. Red or amber stain can sometimes be found, with and without cuttings. There was no Hotel set made. Not marked. Crystal only. Catalog reprint courtesy Neila & Tom Bredehoft.

No. 1200, Cut Block Individual S&C. Catalog reprint courtesy John Martinez. Only the individual sugar and creamer can be found in the custard colored opaque glass that Heisey called Ivorina Verde. Often decorated as souvenir pieces, these are early Heisey S&C which can be found without difficulty. However, it is very difficult to find a sugar and creamer with matching decorations. Note the Ivorina Verde sugars can have a flare to the rim which isn't represented in the illustration above. While it is believed that production of this S&C ceased in 1903, souvenir pieces can be found with dates stretching beyond that. Crystal sets are found with red stain and plain crystal sets are the most difficult to find.

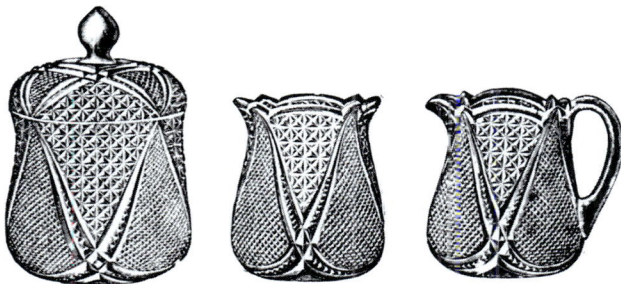

*No. 1201, Fandango Table S&C with spooner (above), Hotel and Individual sets (below). Fandango is also known by the collector's name: **Diamond Swag**. Not marked. Crystal only. 1896-1905.*

No. 1200, Cut Block Individual S&C in Ivorina Verde. Courtesy Dennis Headrick.

No. 1205, Fancy Loop Table sugar and creamer. Courtesy Anonymous.

No. 1220, Punty Band Table set. Courtesy Dennis Headrick.

No. 1205, Fancy Loop *Table S&C with spooner (above) and Hotel set (below). An Individual set was produced which has a similar profile to the Hotel set (see photo). Pieces in this line were made in both crystal and emerald green but to date, the Individual size is the only known S&C to appear in emerald. 1896-1905.*

No. 1220, Punty Band *Table S&C with spooner (above) and Hotel set (below). An Individual set was produced which has a similar profile to the Hotel set shown. The tiny Individual S&C are very difficult to locate. Crystal only. 1896-1909.*

No. 1205, Fancy Loop Hotel size next to Individual size. Photo courtesy Dennis Headrick.

No. 1220, Punty Band Individual creamer was sold without a matching sugar. These standalone creamers were made in crystal, Opal (white), and Ivorina Verde. Courtesy Dennis Headrick.

No. 1250, Groove & Slash Table set. No other size was made. Crystal only. 1898-1906.

No. 1250, Groove & Slash. Courtesy Dennis Headrick.

No. 1225, Plain Band Table S&C with spooner (catalog above), Hotel and Individual S&C (bottom). Crystal only. The Table set can be found with cuttings, gold trim and colored stains. 1896-1905. A "Toy" Table set was also made (below). This is the only toy-sized S&C known to have been made by Heisey. Both photos below courtesy Dennis Headrick.

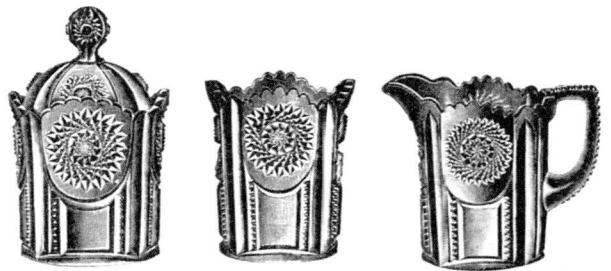

No. 1235, Beaded Panel & Sunburst Table S&C with spooner (above) and Hotel set (below). An Individual set was produced which has a similar profile to the Hotel set shown. Beaded Panel & Sunburst is also known by the collector's name: Chrysanthemum. Crystal only but colored stains or gold decorations are possible. 1896-1913.

No. 150, Pointed Oval in Diamond Point Table S&C with spooner.
Only one size was made. The spooner and sugar are very similar, so you
will need to be careful when purchasing. All of the pieces, including the
creamer, have an inner rim that helps magnify the confusion between the
sugar and the spooner. The sugar lid will not fit the spooner. Typical
sugars are 3 1/8" to 3 1/4" tall while spooners are typically 3 3/8" tall.
Colors include crystal and emerald green. Gold decorations are
possible. 1896-1906. This is one of two Heisey sugar and creamer sets
which are known as No. 150 (see also No. 150, Banded Flute.)
Photo above courtesy Dennis Headrick.

No. 160, Locket on Chain Table S&C with spooner. No other size was
made. Colors include crystal, opal, and emerald green. A spooner is
known to exist in Canary (vaseline).
Colored stains and gold accents are possible. 1896-1910.

No. 1255, Pineapple & Fan Table S&C with spooner (above) and Hotel
set (below). No Individual set was made. Sets can be found in crystal and
Emerald Green. Gold decorations are possible. 1898-1907. Pieces can
be found where the pattern is overcut and polished. The ovecut pieces
feel somewhat like cut glass and can be confused for such.

No. 305, Punty and Diamond Point in Table, Hotel and Individual
sizes (above and below). Crystal only. 1899-1912.
Both photos courtesy John Martinez.

No. 1255, Pineapple & Fan Table set. Courtesy Dennis Headrick.

No. 310, Ring Band Table S&C. No other size was made. Ivorina Verde is the only known color. While this example shows only gold dots, examples where the whole exterior ring is painted gold are known. 1898-1904. Courtesy Anonymous

No. 1295, Bead Swag painted Opal spooner and creamer. Courtesy Karen Plott.

No. 1295, Bead Swag Table S&C with spooner. No other size was made. Colors include crystal, Opal (milk glass), and emerald green. Various decorations are possible but this line is known for hand-painted floral decorations. 1899-1905.

No. 1295, Bead Swag in emerald green. Courtesy Dennis Headrick.

No. 1280, Winged Scroll Table S&C with spooner. No other size was made. Note the sugar is wider and the handles sit lower than the spooner. There is no rim for the lid. The lid has an extended bottom that sits down into the sugar. Colors made were crystal, emerald green, Opal and Ivorina Verde. A rare Table set is known to exist in Canary (vaseline). Crystal is more difficult to find than green. Opal is very scarce. Most sugars and creamers were originally decorated with gold accents, occasionally you'll find painted floral decorations. 1898-1904.

No. 325, Pillows *Table S&C with spooner (above).*
A squat Hotel sugar (below) is shown in the catalogs. It's reasonable to
assume that a Hotel creamer may have also been made; but no catalog
drawing exists and no creamer has ever been found. If the Hotel creamer
exists, it's shape would likely be similar to the No. 335, Prince of Wales
Plumes Hotel creamer shown further below. Crystal only. 1901-1912.

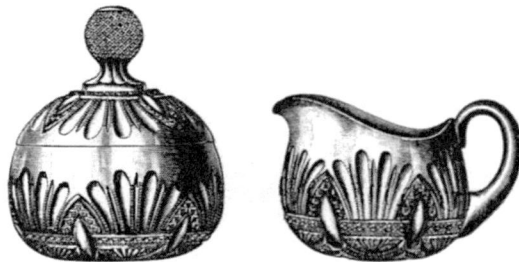

No. 335, Prince of Wales Plumes *Hotel S&C (above) and Table S&C*
with spooner (below). Crystal only. Gold and ruby stain decorations
are known. 1902-1912.

No. 343, Sunburst *Table S&C with spooner (above) and Hotel set*
(below). An Individual set was produced which has a similar profile to
the Hotel set shown. The Hotel and Individual sets are oval in shape.
Crystal only. 1903-1920.

No 343, Sunburst oval Hotel S&C. Courtesy Dennis Headrick.

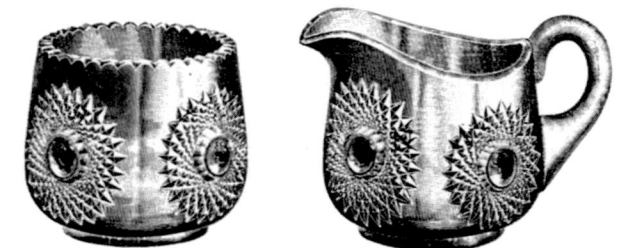

No. 343 1/2, Sunburst *round Hotel set. Very unusual set, rarely seen.*
Crystal only. Early 1900s.

No. 1776, Kalonyal *Table S&C with spooner (above) and Hotel S&C (below). Crystal only. 1905-1907.*

No. 379, Urn *Table S&C with spooner (above) and Hotel S&C (below). Note the Hotel sugar was sold with and without a lid. The same lid fits both the Table and Hotel sugars. Crystal only. 1907-1911.*

No. 397, Colonial Cupped Scallop *Table S&C with spooner. This set did not appear in any known catalogs. However, it did appear in Heisey advertising. No other size is believed to have been made. Crystal only. Circa 1910. Courtesy Dennis Hecdrick.*

No. 337, Touraine Table S&C with spooner. No other size was made. Sugar and spooner are very similar, so compare carefully. Crystal only. Decorations include colored stains, gold and banding. 1902-1938.

No. 350, Pinwheel and Fan Hotel S&C. No other size was made. Crystal only. 1908-1945. Sets are known where the pattern is overcut and polished. The overcut pieces feel somewhat like cut glass and can be confused for such.

No. 365, Queen Ann Table S&C with spooner (above) and Hotel S&C (below). Crystal only. 1907-1911. This is one of two Heisey sugar and creamer sets which are known as Queen Ann (see also No. 1509, Queen Ann.)

No. 423, Diamond Band Table S&C with spooner. No other size was made. Crystal only. 1910-1913. Catalog reprint courtesy Dennis Headrick.

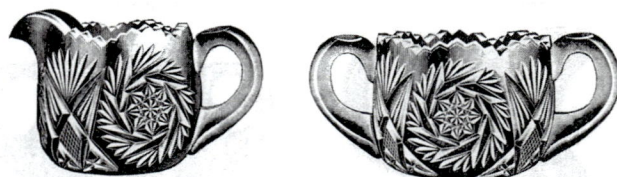

No. 427, Daisy and Leaves Hotel S&C. No other size was made. Crystal only. 1910. Courtesy John Martinez.

No. 365, Queen Ann Hotel S&C. Courtesy Anonymous.

No. 439, Raised Loop Hotel S&C. No other size was made. Crystal only. 1911-1915.

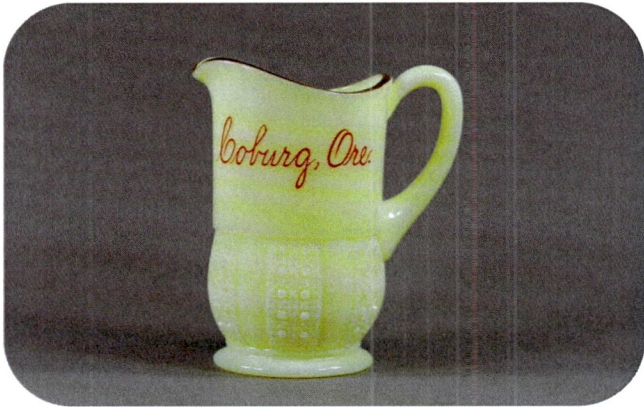

No. 8047, Cane and Bar 1/4 pint (4 oz.) souvenir creamer in Ivorina
Verde. No matching sugar has ever been found. Examples can be found
with painted roses, similar to the style of painting found on No. 1200,
Cut Block. The creamer stands about 4' tall.
Circa late 1890s to early 1900s.

In the early years of the company, Heisey produced a small selection of standalone creamers which many S&C collectors enjoy adding to their collections. All photos this page courtesy Dennis Headrick.

Nos. 1200, Cut Block 7 oz. Tankard creamer and
5 oz. tall creamer, both with red stain.

No. 1220, Punty Band 4 oz. creamer with red stain.

No. 1255, Pineapple and Fan 4 oz. creamers in crystal
with red stain and in Opal. Also known in Ivorina Verde.

Pricing for the early Heisey pieces shown prior to this point is not provided. This is due partially to a lack of available information; but also to the lack of available space to do justice to the nuances surrounding the various decorations. For example, it's difficult to set one price for gold trimmed items because sometimes the location of the gold makes one item more valuable than another. Many of these early pieces are too rare to price (trtp), but not all. Keep your eyes open and you can add some of these sets to your collection without too much effort or money. Watch online Heisey auctions and see what other bidders get excited about. It won't take long to get a feel for how much some of these items are worth.

Heisey is very well known for their colonial styled S&C. So much so that those who do not consult any reference books will identify any crystal S&C with colonial styling as Heisey.

Pleated design element around the base known as the "petticoat".

No. 300, Peerless *Table S&C with spooner (above), Hotel and Individual S&C (below). Crystal only. 1897-1938.*

*Of all the colonial S&C sets, No. 300, Peerless was the longest running and many Heisey sets which followed copied elements of it's classic design. One of the Peerless characteristics is a pleated ring around the underside of the bowl. Collectors refer to this design element as a petticoat. At some point the petticoats were removed but it's unclear exactly when. After the Peerless Table set was discontinued, the Hotel and Individual sizes remained in the catalogs for many years. In the late 1930s, both of these sets became part of the **No. 341, Old Williamsburg** line. Old Williamsburg was produced until Heisey shut it's doors in 1957. Following the Heisey closure, Imperial Glass continued to produce the No. 300 Hotel and Individual sets under the name of Old Williamsburg in crystal and colors. Almost immediately, Imperial changed the Hotel sugar by adding a rim, and sold their Hotel set with a lid. Heisey never sold the Hotel set with a lid. For clarification in this book, these pieces will always be referred to as No. 300.*

The individual Peerless set appears in most antique malls and flea markets multiple times. This S&C is found in crystal, multiple colors and with a red stain. Many of these small sets which are being sold as Heisey were instead made by either Canton Glass or Imperial Glass companies. At some point in the mid-century, Canton began to sell their No. 450, 2-1/2 oz. Individual S&C set and it probably wasn't a coincidence that Canton also called their set "Peerless" (see Canton chapter in Book 1). Canton pieces have a weakly defined sawtooth rim, chunkier handles, and the horizontal ridge element at the base of the flutes is straight. Heisey and Imperial pieces have a slight scallop at their base (see the area highlighted in red above: Heisey No. 300, Peerless at left. Canton No. 450, Peerless at right.) Canton sets are found in crystal, crystal with red stain, and cobalt.
Ironically, Imperial sets also can have weakly defined sawteeth and eventually the sawtooth rim disappeared completely from their pieces. Imperial colors are: crystal, amber, Azalea, Blue Haze (medium blue), Nut Brown, Rose Pink, Sunshine Yellow, Ultra Blue (cobalt) and Verde green (avocado). Watch for the scallop at the base, Imperial never modified that and it's a sure-fire way to identify Canton pieces in the crowd of Peerless and Old Williamsburg.

No. 300 1/2, Peerless Table S&C with spooner (above) and footed Hotel S&C (below). Table sugars and spooners are very similar. Crystal only. 1899-1938. The footed Hotel set is a striking, yet relatively common and inexpensive set for collectors who are looking to add an iconic Colonial Heisey sugar and creamer to their collection.

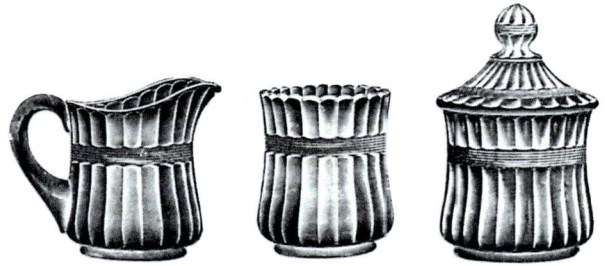

No. 150, Banded Flute Table S&C with spooner (above) and Hotel S&C (below). The spooner has a scalloped rim in the catalog illustration but only flat-rimmed spooners have ever been found. Be aware, the spooner is the same diameter as the Hotel sugar and spooners are sometimes found underneath the Hotel lid. The spooner is taller than the Hotel sugar and will be too tall for the Hotel creamer. Crystal only. 1908-1933. This is the second set to use the No. 150 designation. (See also No. 150, Pointed Oval in Diamond Point.)

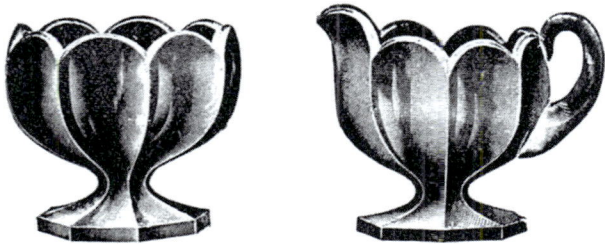

No. 315, Paneled Cane Table S&C with spooner. Crystal only. 1900-1908. Courtesy Dennis Headrick.

No. 339 1/2, Continental footed Table S&C with spooner. 1903-1944. Courtesy Dennis Headrick.

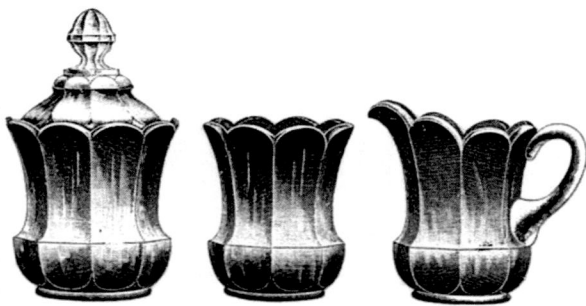

*No. 339, Continental Table S&C with spooner (above) and
Hotel S&C (below right). Crystal only. 1903-1944.
Catalog reprint courtesy Neila & Tom Bredehoft.*

No. 339, Continental Table sugar. Courtesy Anonymous.

No. 339, Continental Hotel S&C. Courtesy Anonymous.

No. 341, Puritan footed Table S&C with spooner (above) and oval Hotel S&C (below). Tall footed sugars like this are often confused with candy jars. Crystal only. 1904-1938. This is not the only time Heisey used No. 341 as a line number. (See also No. 341, Old Williamsburg.)

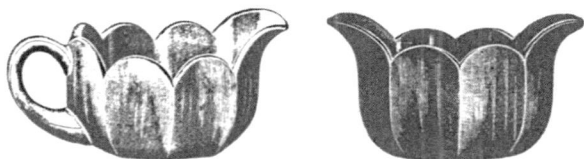

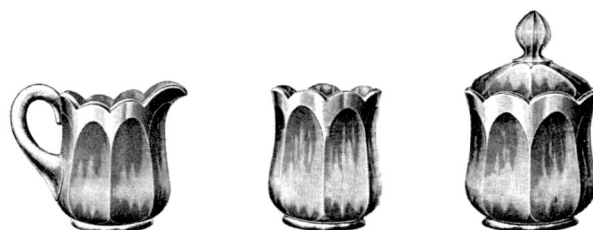

No. 341 1/2, Puritan Table S&C with spooner (above) and No. 342, Paneled Colonial Table S&C with spooner (below). Although the catalog illustrations shown vary slightly, some Heisey collectors believe that these two Table sets may be the same. The difference between the two sets lies with the different butters which were sold with each (not shown). No. 341 1/2 was in the catalogs from 1904-1938 while No. 342 was only in the 1906 catalog. After 1938, the No. 341 1/2 creamer and spooner continued in the catalogs for a time as the No. 341 creamer and open sugar. Crystal only.

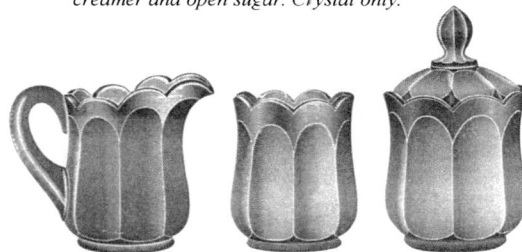

No. 341, Puritan footed Table S&C with spooner. Courtesy Dennis Headrick.

No. 400, Colonial Scallop Top Hotel S&C. Crystal only. 1905-1915.

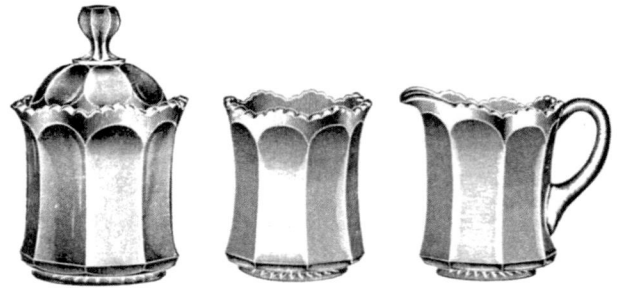

No. 400, Colonial Scallop Top Table S&C with spooner. Because there is no inner rim for the lid, the sugar ribs are flat topped on the inside; this supports the lid. The lack of rim for the lid leads some to mistake the sugar for a spooner. At least one unusual creamer is known which has one less large scallop at the top of the ribs, making a more elongated creamer spout instead.

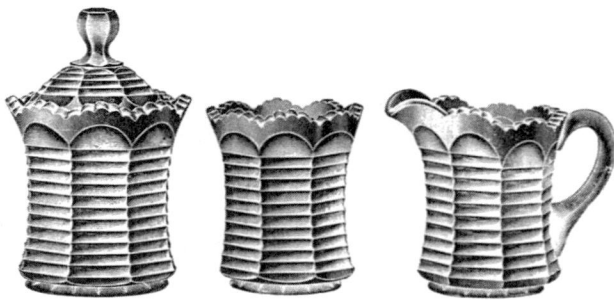

No. 357, Prison Stripe *Table S&C with spooner (above) and Hotel S&C catalog reprint (below). Despite the catalog reprint shown, the Hotel sugar with handles may have never been made. Hotel sugars found today do not have handles (see photo at bottom). The handle-less Hotel sugar is the same configuration as the similar No.400, Colonial Scallop Top. Crystal only. 1904-1909.*

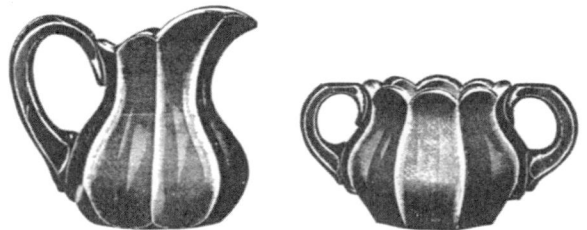

No. 351, Priscilla *flat cut-shut Hotel S&C (above) and flared Hotel S&C (below). The flared set was sold with and without 6 1/2" round under plates. The cut-shut set is scarce while the flared S&C is one of the more easily found pre-Depression sets available for today's collector. The level of flaring varies from pronounced to nearly vertically straight. The plates are difficult to find. Crystal only. 1905-1933.*

No. 357, Prison Stripe Hotel S&C. Courtesy Dennis Headrick.

6 1/2" Under plate for No. 351, Priscilla flared Hotel S&C.

No. 352, **Flat Panel** Hotel S&C (above) and Individual S&C (below). Both of these sets were sold with and without the sugar lid and lids can be difficult to locate. The individual sugar became a mustard with the addition of a slotted lid. Crystal only. Both sets can be found with elaborate silver overlays. 1907-1920.
In the 1950s, the No. 352, Flat Panel Hotel set made a reappearance without it's lid on catalog pages specifically for the Hotel-trade.

No. 353, **Medium Flat Panel** oval Hotel S&C. Crystal only. 1909-1935. This set is frequently found with cuttings.

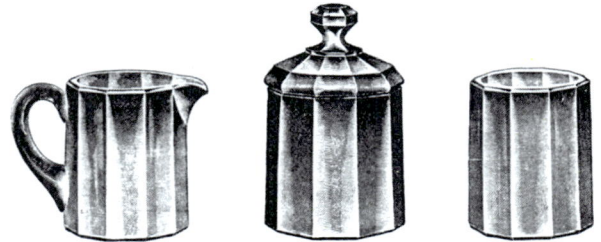

No. 353, **Medium Flat Panel** round Table S&C with spooner (above) and round Hotel S&C (below). Table sugars and spooners are the same height but the diameters are different. Both the Table and Hotel sugars are the same diameter and they share the same lid. Crystal only.

Courtesy Ted Sheets & John Martinez.

The No. 354, **Wide Flat Panel** stacking set (above left) had a close cousin: No. 356, **Wide Flat Panel** stacking set (above right). Both sets used the same creamer. The No. 354 sugar had two handles and the No. 356 sugar had none. Both sugars and the creamer were sold individually, individually with the butter-pat, and as a 3-piece set. Both sets were introduced in 1913 with No. 356 being discontinued almost immediately. The No. 354 S&C was the only stacking set made in color, and they only made it in Flamingo. The pink S&C is difficult to locate but the major prize is the pink butter-pat lid. 1913-1937.

*No. 354, **Wide Flat Panel** footed oval Hotel S&C. One of the first sugar and creamer sets to be offered in the four colors of Flamingo, Moongleam, Hawthorne and Sahara. Moongleam and Flamingo were first available in the mid 1920s. Hawthorne was only made during the years of 1927-1928, and Sahara was introduced in 1930. Crystal pieces were available from 1913-1937. Crystal sets can be found with a variety of decorations and the occasional colored set is found with cuttings. Photos below shows Hawthorne creamer next to Flamingo sugar.*

*No. 429, **Plain Panel Recess** Hotel S&C. No other sizes were made. This is a heavy, thick-walled set. Look for the sloped bottom. Crystal only. 1910-1925.*

*No. 465, **Recessed Panel** S&C. No other sizes were made. The sugar is the same as the 1/4 lb. candy jar. Crystal only. 1915-1933. Photo courtesy Dennis Headrick. Catalog reprint courtesy Neila & Tom Bredehoft.*

*No. 451, **Cross Lined Flute** Hotel footed sugar. No creamer is listed. The type of sugar which resembles a large sherbet or a footed compote is known by the collector's name: English sugar. Very difficult to find. Crystal only. 1917.*

No. 393, **Narrow Flute** round Hotel S&C. Crystal only. Original line issued from 1909-1944. Courtesy Kay & Dave Tucker.

No. 393, Narrow Flute round Table S&C with spooner. Crystal only. Note the creamer in the catalog illustration above is squattier than the actual creamer shown below. Photo courtesy Dennis Headrick.

No. 393, Narrow Flute Individual S&C. Colors made were Flamingo, Moongleam and Sahara. Rare sugars are found in Marigold and a few blue creamers are known. Photos courtesy Ted Sheets & John Martinez.

No. 393, Narrow Flute footed oval Hotel S&C. One of the more easily found S&C sets even though it was discontinued before 1929. Crystal only but many sets can be found decorated. Shown below with enamel flowers and gold trim (sugar used to highlight decoration).

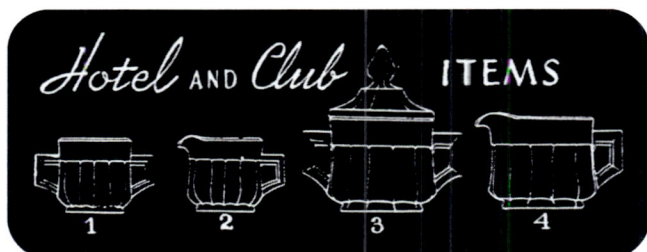

Size comparison between No. 393 round Hotel sugar and Individual sugar (above). Courtesy Kay & Dave Tucker. During the 1950s, both of these sizes of Narrow Flute were reissued in crystal for the hotel market (see 1953 catalog illustration below).

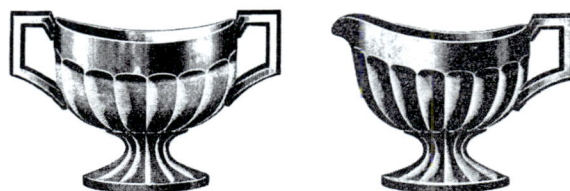

Hotel AND *Club* ITEMS

1   2   3   4

*No. 406, **Coarse Rib** Hotel S&C in Hawthorne. Although researchers have identified this as part of the Course Rib line, Heisey advertising in 1923 called the set **Colonial Fluted**. Sets were sold with and without the sugar lid. Other colors made were Flamingo and Moongleam. 1923-1937. Courtesy Ted Sheets & John Martinez.*

*No. 407, **Coarse Rib** Hotel S&C (above and below). Crystal only. 1923-1937. Courtesy Ted Sheets & John Martinez.*

No. 406, Course Rib sugars. Courtesy Kay & Dave Tucker.

No. 407, Coarse Rib Individual S&C (above and below). Crystal only. Courtesy Dennis Headrick.

*No. 417, **Double Rib & Panel** Hotel S&C. Crystal only. Very difficult to locate. 1923-1937. Photo courtesy Anonymous.*

No. 472, Narrow Flute with Rim stacking S&C with butter pat lid.
Crystal only. Mid-1910s to early 1930s.
Photos (above and right) courtesy Kay & Dave Tucker.

No. 473, Narrow Flute with Rim Hotel S&C (above) and
Individual S&C (below). Crystal only. 1915-1933.

No. 473, Narrow Flute with Rim Hotel set decorated with blue enamel
and gold. The Hotel S&C was sold with and without the lid.
Courtesy Dave Lippert.

Shown below are the two sizes of No. 473 Narrow Flute with Rim
domino sugar sets. The larger or "Loaf" sugar size has a tray diameter
of 6-3/8" (does not include handles) and holds a 4-oz. creamer which is
nearly 3-1/2" tall. The smaller "Dice" set has a tray diameter of 5-3/8"
and holds a 3-oz. creamer which is 3" tall.

No. 473, Narrow Flute with Rim domino sets were first manufactured in 1915 and continued into the mid-1920s. Many can be found with a patent date embossed on the bottom of the tray. Dice and Loaf sets are found with partial or complete colored stains. Partially stained sets are lightly iridized. In addition to crystal, Dice sets can be found in an early darker shade of Moongleam. Courtesy Kay & Dave Tucker.

Dice sugar with unique gold and enamel-painted tray. Unknown decorating company. Courtesy Kay & Dave Tucker.

Dice tray in darker Moongleam. Courtesy Ted Sheets & John Martinez.

Trays found without the inner ring are identified in the catalogs as the 5" two-handled jelly and the 6" two-handled cheese tray.

Gold encrusted Loaf tray showing loaf sugar placement. The term "Domino" refers to the Domino sugar company which sold sugar cubes. A "Loaf" sugar cube is rectangular in shape and a "Dice" sugar cube is a smaller square shape. Courtesy Dennis Headrick.

Side by side comparison between Westmoreland amber Domino set (left) and No. 473, Marigold stained Domino set (right). Indiana and Paden City Glass companies also made similar Domino sets but no other set has the distinctive narrow ribs of the Heisey set. Courtesy Dave Lippert.

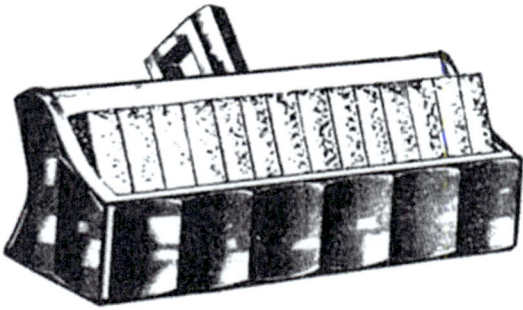

No. 354, Wide Flat Panel "single-bench" Domino sugar. 1913-1937.

No. 354, Wide Flat Panel, combination Domino sugar and spoon tray.

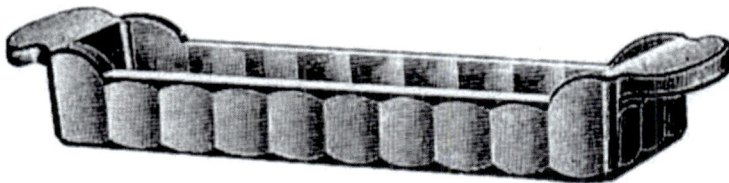

No. 393, Narrow Flute
Domino sugar. 1909-1944.
Heisey advertisements showed
this tiny sugar holder on a
breakfast tray accompanied by
the No. 353 Hotel creamer.
Photo above shows No. 393 in
comparison to a US quarter.
Courtesy Dave Lippert.

DOMINO SUGAR
PATENT NO. 45893

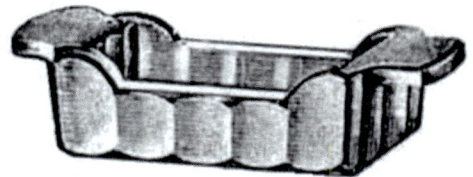

INDIVIDUAL DOMINO SUGAR
PATENT NO. 45893

No. 394, Narrow Flute, Domino sugar and Individual Domino sugar
trays. The larger tray is known in crystal, Moongleam, Flamingo and
Sahara. 1909-1944.

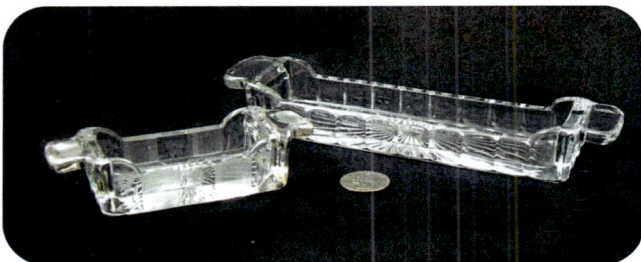

Size comparison to US quarter. Courtesy Kay & Dave Tucker.

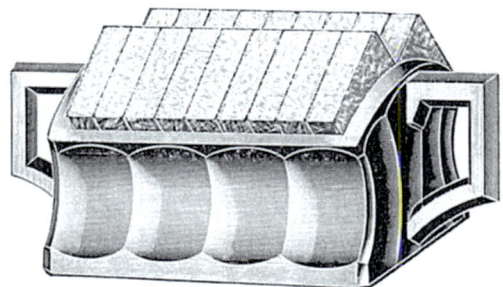

No 355, Quator, two-sided "double bench" Domino sugar showing
placement of loaf-shaped sugar cubes inside tray. 1906-1938.

No. 433, Greek Key round Table S&C with spooner (above) and round Hotel S&C (below). Table sugars and spooners are similar and spooners are significantly more common than the sugars. Watch the diameter as the sugars have no rim for a lid. The finial on the lid is frequently found damaged, so check carefully should you be lucky enough to find one. The Hotel set is not as tapered as it appears in the catalog drawing (see photo below.) Crystal only. Gold and silver overlay is occasionally found on the "key" design. 1912-1938.

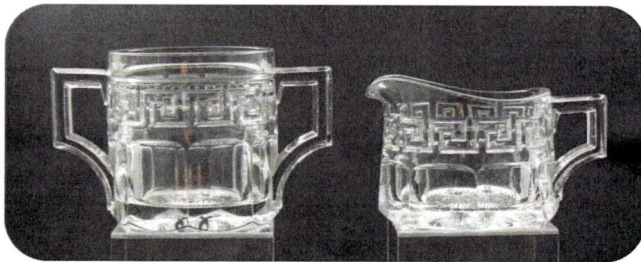

Size comparison between No. 433, Greek Key round Table sugar and round Hotel creamer. Courtesy Kay & Dave Tucker.

No. 433, Greek Key oval Hotel S&C (above) and oval Individual S&C (below). Notice the spout difference between the round sets (left) and these oval sets. Round sets have the spout pulled up from the rim and oval sets have the spouts pulled forward.

No. 358 is an unnamed Hotel S&C. The lidded sugar appears to be the same mold as the No. 352, Flat Panel marmalade, only the lid doesn't have the slot for a spoon. Crystal only. Probably made from the mid-1910s to 1920. Catalog reprint courtesy Neila & Tom Bredehoft.

Heisey	Crystal Sugar with lid	Crystal Creamer or lidless sugar	Other
#150, Banded Flute Table	trtp	trtp	
#150, Banded Flute Hotel	trtp	trtp	
#300, Peerless Table	trtp	trtp	
#300, Peerless Hotel		$10	
#300, Peerless Individual		$8	2x for pieces with petticoat
#300 1/2, Peerless Table	trtp	trtp	
#300 1/2, Peerless Hotel		$10	
#315, Paneled Cane Table	trtp	trtp	
#339, Continental Table	trtp	trtp	
#339, Continental Hotel		trtp	
#339 1/2, Continental Table	trtp	trtp	

Heisey	Crystal Sugar with lid	Crystal Creamer or lidless sugar	Other
#341, Puritan Table	trtp	trtp	
#341, Puritan Hotel oval		$18	
#341 1/2, Puritan Table	trtp	trtp	
#342, Paneled Colonial Table	trtp	trtp	
#351, Priscilla Hotel cut shut	trtp	trtp	
#351, Priscilla Hotel flared	$12	$12	$20 under plate
#352, Flat Panel Hotel	$25 +	$14 +	
#352, Flat Panel Individual	$45 +	$22 +	
#353, Medium Flat Panel Table	trtp	trtp	
#353, Medium Flat Panel Hotel	trtp	trtp	
#353, Medium Flat Panel Hotel oval		$9 +	
#354, Wide Flat Panel Hotel		$9 +	$22 yellow, $26 pink, $33 green, $45 Hawthorne
#354, Wide Flat Panel Individual stacking	$15 (w/ butter pat)	$8	$24 sugar or creamer (pink), $36 butter pat (pink)
#354, Wide Flat Panel bench domino sugar		$30	$18 domino with spoon rest
#355, Quator double bench domino sugar		trtp	
#356, Wide Flat Panel Individual stacking		trtp	
#357, Prison Stripe Table	trtp	trtp	
#357, Prison Stripe Hotel		trtp	
#358, Hotel	trtp	trtp	
#393, Narrow Flute Table	trtp	trtp	
#393, Narrow Flute Hotel round	$12	$8	
#393, Narrow Flute Hotel footed oval		$11 +	
#393, Narrow Flute Individual		$7	$24 pink, $35 green, $55 yellow
#393, Narrow Flute domino sugar		$24 +	
#394, Narrow Flute domino sugar large		$28	all colors trtp
#394, Narrow Flute domino sugar small		$40	
#400, Colonial Scalloped Top Table	trtp	trtp	
#400, Colonial Scalloped Top Hotel	trtp	trtp	
#406, Coarse Rib Hotel	sugar w/ lid, crystal trtp, pink $28, green $30, Hawthorne $46		
	creamer, crystal trtp, pink $15, green $20, Hawthorne $40		
#407, Coarse Rib Hotel	trtp	$18	
#407, Coarse Rib Individual		trtp	
#417, Double Rib & Panel Hotel	trtp	trtp	
#429, Plain Panel Recess Hotel	trtp	trtp	
#433, Greek Key Table round	trtp	trtp	
#433, Greek Key Hotel oval		$16	
#433, Greek Key Hotel round		trtp	
#433, Greek Key Individual oval		trtp	
#451, Cross Lined Flute Hotel		trtp	
#465, Recessed Panel Hotel	trtp	trtp	
#472, Narrow Flute with Rim Individual stacking	trtp (with butter pat)	trtp	
#473, Narrow Flute with Rim Hotel	trtp	trtp	
#473, Narrow Flute with Rim Individual		trtp	
#473, Narrow Flute with Rim domino large		$16 +	tray $16 +
#473, Narrow Flute with Rim domino small		$18 +	tray $20 +, Moongleam sets are trtp

+ Add 50% to 3x for decorated pieces, depending on scarcity, condition and desirability.

*No. 355, **Quator** Hotel and Individual S&C sets. Note the catalog illustration shows a swirl in the base. Actual pieces have a star in the base. The Hotel set is widely available in plain and decorated crystal. One of the more unusual decorations has the rim notched by a cutting wheel into a sawtooth design. Availability of the Individual set is another story. Plain or decorated, it is scarce and you should purchase this set when you see it. Crystal only. 1906-1938.*

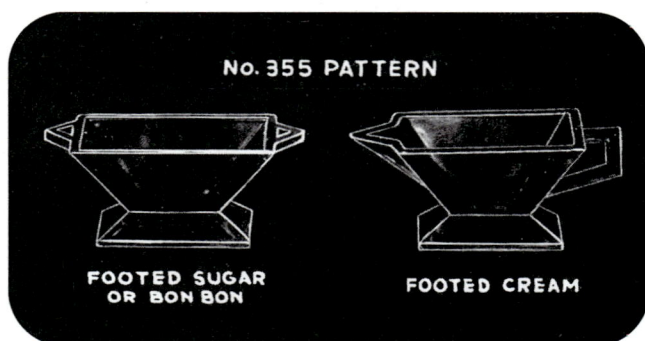

NO. 355 PATTERN

FOOTED SUGAR
OR BON BON

FOOTED CREAM

*No. 355, Quator footed Hotel S&C (above & below). This is the only Quator set that comes in colors. Sets can be found in crystal, Flamingo, Moongleam, Sahara and the elusive Marigold.
Photo courtesy Ted Sheets & John Martinez.*

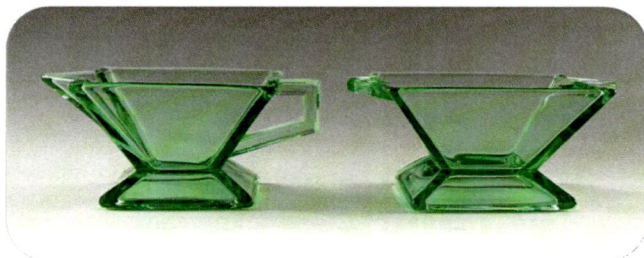

*No. 1180, **Debra** Hotel S&C (above & below). Crystal only. 1919-1935. Many sets can be found decorated. Sold with and without a lid. This lid is similar to the lid which was sold with the No. 1183 1/2, Revere sugar.*

No. 1180, Debra Hotel S&C with gold overlaid etching.

No. 452
HOTEL SUGAR
CUT TOP AND BOTTOM

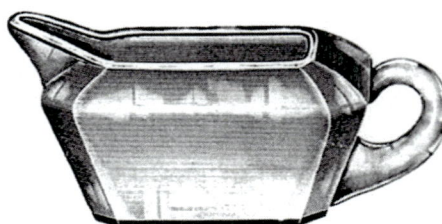

No. 452
HOTEL CREAM
CUT TOP AND BOTTOM

No. 452, no name. Crystal only. 1915. A rare set of which little information is known. Note it has a "cut" top and bottom.

No.1181, Revere Individual S&C (above & below). Crystal only. 1914-1928. Notice the sugar has pressed handles and a thin cut-shut base while the creamer has a thicker, ground and polished base and a "stuck" handle. In addition, the creamer is slightly smaller than the sugar. Courtesy Ted Sheets & John Martinez.

No. 1183, Revere Individual S&C (above) and No. 1183 1/2, Revere Individual lidded sugar (below). Both photos courtesy Ted Sheets & John Martinez.

No. 1182, Revere is a tall, somewhat A-shaped creamer which was thought to be a standalone piece for many years. All the known Heisey catalogs have shown it as such. Recently the set below surfaced indicating that at least for a short time, Heisey made a sugar which was paired with the lonely bachelor. The sugar echoes the A-shape of the creamer and is slightly taller than the No. 1181 sugar. Crystal only. 1914-1928. Courtesy Ted Sheets & John Martinez.

Both the Nos. 1183 and 1183 1/2, Revere Individual sugars were sold with the same No. 1183 creamer. A wide variety of cuttings and silver overlays can be found on all the individual Revere sets. Crystal only. 1914-1928.

Nos. 1182 creamer (left) and 1183 creamer (right) for comparison. Courtesy Dennis Headrick.

*No. 1183, Revere tall footed Hotel S&C. Sugar is made from
a 1/4-lb. candy jar. The creamer is a candy with a stuck handle and a
pulled out spout. Crystal only. 1914-1928.
Catalog reprint courtesy Neila & Tom Bredehoft.*

*No. 1183, Revere oval Hotel set. Crystal only. The large, almost flat
surfaces of this S&C made it ideal for decorating and you will find a
wide variety of cuttings. Courtesy Ted Sheets & John Martinez.*

*The set above may be part of the Revere line. No catalog reference has
been found and the Heisey Museum displays the set as part of the Revere
line. Courtesy Dennis Headrick.*

*No. 485, Dunham Table S&C. A short-lived, crystal only set from 1917.
Dunham is rare and sets with elaborate cuttings are known.
Catalog reprint courtesy Neila & Tom Bredehoft.*

*The S&C above is known as No. 8061, Lodi. The 8000 number series is
assigned by Heisey Collectors of America when they can not find any
other reference. Some researchers believe this set could be
No. 1188, Yeoman oval footed Hotel S&C. Crystal only. Circa 1920s.
Photo courtesy Ted Sheets & John Martinez.*

*No. 479, Petal Hotel S&C. 1917-1929. Colors include crystal,
Flamingo, Hawthorne, Moongleam, and Sahara. The 1917 price list
indicates that the crystal sugar was sold with and without a lid. The only
known crystal lids have a spoon notch which begs the question, Did the
sugar lid have a notch or is there a notch-less lid out there?*

No. 1184, Yeoman round Individual stacking S&C with butter pat lid.
Crystal only. 1913-1957. Courtesy Ted Sheets & John Martinez.

No. 1184, Yeoman Individual stacking S&C. Courtesy Karen Plott.

No. 1184—Individual Butter

No. 1184—Individual Cream

No. 1184—Individual Sugar

No. 1184—Combination Sugar, Cream and Butter

No. 1185—Individual Cream

No. 1185—Individual Sugar

No. 1185—Hotel Cream

No. 1185—Hotel Sugar

No 1184, Yeoman Individual stacking S&C (left) and No. 1185, Yeoman Hotel and Individual sets (right). The Yeoman sugars resemble some of the No. 1183, Revere sugars and the two lines are easily confused. In addition, other glass companies produced lookalike round-handled sugars and creamers but I've yet to uncover any other company which used the same prominent spout which the Heisey Yeoman pieces have.

No. 1185, Yeoman Hotel round S&C. Crystal only. 1913-1957.

No. 1185, Yeoman Individual round S&C. Crystal only.
Courtesy Ted Sheets & John Martinez.

*Originally introduced around 1915, the **No. 1023** Hotel S&C appeared in catalogs on a page of standalone Hotel sugar and creamer sets. Crystal only. Photo courtesy Ted Sheets & John Martinez.*

*Eventually the set was added to the Yeoman line and given the identity of **No. 1184**. You can see in the photo above that No. 1023 has a star in it's base. As the set became part of the Yeoman line, the star was removed. Also, once the set became Yeoman, catalogs show that it was made in both a plain and diamond optic version. Today, the diamond optic pieces are much more plentiful than the non-optic pieces.*

No. 1184, Yeoman, Diamond optic. Colors available are crystal, Moongleam, Flamingo, Sahara, Hawthorne and Marigold. Creamer below has no diamond optic. Compare the distortion above the bases of the Marigold and Hawthorne sets shown to the lack of distortion in the round glass of the pink piece. The lid has no optic.
Photos above and below, courtesy Ted Sheets & John Martinez.

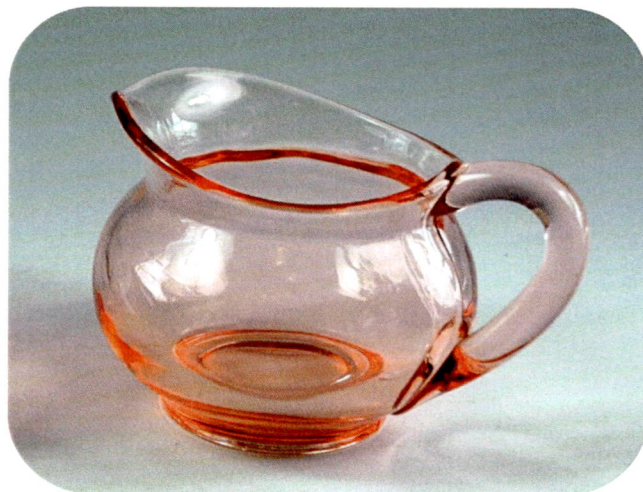

No. 1184, Yeoman round Hotel S&C with diamond optic in Hawthorne with No. 440 Frontenec etching. Courtesy Dave Lippert.

No. 1184, Yeoman mustard and Individual creamer. Not really a S&C set but the creamer has no matching sugar and some collectors display these two pieces together as a marriage. This is a tiny set with the pieces coming in just under 3" without the lid. Available in crystal, Flamingo, Moongleam, and Sahara. 1913-1957.
Courtesy Ted Sheets & John Martinez.

No. 1189, Yeoman footed Individual S&C (above & below). Available in crystal, Moongleam, Flamingo and Sahara. Ironically, crystal is the most difficult color to locate. 1925-1937.
Photo above courtesy Kay & Dave Tucker.
Photo below courtesy Dennis Headrick.

No. 1186, Yeoman footed oval Hotel S&C. Crystal only but this set can be found with a wide variety of decorations. 1913 to mid-1930s. Set above has satinized bowls with hand-painting and silver trim.
Photo courtesy Dave Lippert.

No. 1190, "no name" oval flat Hotel S&C (above & below). Typically found only in crystal but a rare Flamingo set is known to exist. Circa 1920s.

No. 1020, Phyllis Hotel S&C. A standalone set made from 1920-1933. Colors included crystal, Flamingo, Moongleam, and darker Moongleam. A rare few sets were made in Canary (vaseline). Pieces can be found with simple or elaborate cuttings. Sets can be found with both plain (see Flamingo) and wide optic interiors (see Moongleam).
Photo courtesy Dennis Headrick.

*No. 7068, **Four Arch** footed Hotel S&C (aka **Lokey**). Crystal only. Circa 1920s. This set has an unusual diamond shaped lid. Heisey researcher, Clarence Vogel, assigned the No. 7000 series numbers for reference when the actual line number was not known. Courtesy Ted Sheets & John Martinez.*

No. 360
HOTEL SUGAR AND COVER

No. 360
HOTEL CREAM

*No. 4222, **Horseshoe** S&C. Available in crystal, Flamingo, Sahara, and crystal with Moongleam handles. Horseshoe is unusual in that it was blown in mold and has stuck handles. The opening in the top is hand cut and polished. Because they are blown, this set is one of the few made after 1901 that is not marked. 1931-1937. Courtesy Kay & Dave Tucker.*

*No. 360, **Corby** Hotel S&C. Crystal only. 1922-1935. Corby is not as difficult to find as Lokey, but it is still considered rare; especially with the lid. Sets can be found decorated with cuttings and/or gold trim. Photo at left courtesy Ted Sheets & John Martinez.*

No. 1021, Christine.

No. 1021, Christine *Hotel S&C. A standalone oval set made from 1921-1933. Crystal only.*

No. 1022, Harding. Courtesy Ted Sheets and John Martinez.

No. 1022, Harding *Hotel S&C. A standalone set made from 1921-1933. Crystal only.*

No. 1024, Eileen. Courtesy Dave Lippert.

No. 1024, Eileen *Hotel S&C. A standalone set made from 1922-1933. Crystal only. Set shown at left has a yellow stain, cuttings, and silver trim.*

No. 1025, Sharon. Courtesy Kay & Dave Tucker.

No. 1025, Sharon *Hotel S&C. A standalone round set made from 1922-1933. Crystal only. Set shown at left has the Wheeling No. D-53, Pheasant & Stump decoration in blue enamel and gold etching*

No. 411, Tudor footed Table S&C (above) and No. 411, Tudor Hotel S&C (below). 1923-1939. The footed Table set came in crystal only. The Hotel set came in crystal, Hawthorne, and crystal with Moongleam handles. The Hotel set was sold both with and without a lid.

No. 411, Tudor. Courtesy Kay & Dave Tucker. Set is satinized, has gold etching and trim, enamel paint and a painted crackle treatment.

No. 414, Tudor standalone covered sugar (left). Available in crystal, Flamingo and Hawthorne. 1923-1939. Photo courtesy Ted Sheets & John Martinez.

Catalogs also showed a No. 412 standalone sugar. This piece was the same shape as the No. 411, Hotel sugar and lid, but had no handles. Crystal only.

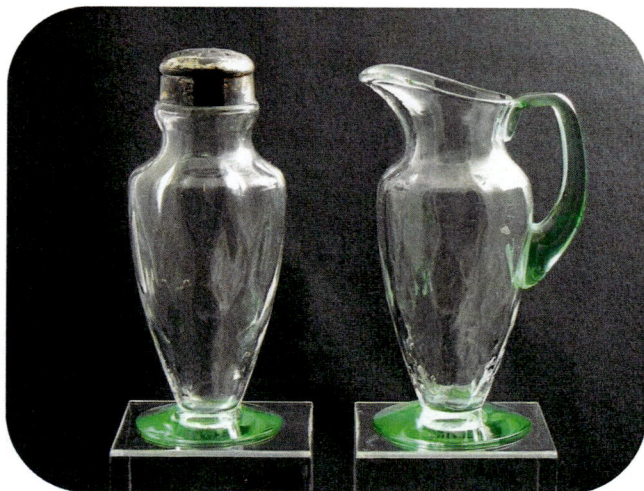

No. 411, Tudor Hotel S&C. Courtesy Ted Sheets & John Martinez.

Shown above is the Lenox S&C from McKee Glass. Lenox looks very similar to Heisey's Tudor even to the little ball at the top of the finial. Overall, the McKee design is chunkier and less defined. Heisey pieces have a pattern of two subtle external ribs while McKee pieces have three. McKee sets are known in crystal and pink.

No. 1001, Casewell sugar sifter with tall creamer. Available in Flamingo, Hawthorne, and crystal with Moongleam handles. Sugars are found with both metal and glass lids. 1925-1933. Courtesy Kay & Dave Tucker.

No. 1252, Twist oval Hotel S&C. Available in crystal, Flamingo, Moongleam, Sahara, and Marigold. This is the only sugar and creamer in this line which came in Sahara and Sahara is the most difficult color to find. Occasionally sets are found with cuttings. 1929-1930. Photo courtesy Ted Sheets & John Martinez.

No. 1252, Twist Individual S&C. Available in crystal, Flamingo, Moongleam, and Marigold. The sugar was additionally sold as a footed almond dish while the creamer was sold as a dressing boat. Courtesy Dennis Headrick.

No. 1252, Twist colors. Courtesy Dennis Headrick.

No. 1252, Twist footed Hotel S&C. Occasionally sets are found with a silver overlay along the top band. Available in crystal, Flamingo, and Moongleam. Courtesy Kay & Dave Tucker.

No. 1252, Twist Hotel S&C with lid is one of the rarest sets from the Depression era. This set is high on the "want" list for most Heisey and S&C collectors. The difficult to grasp handles can be damaged easily, so check them carefully before paying full price. Lids can be very difficult to find. Available in crystal, Flamingo, and Moongleam. Courtesy Ted Sheets and John Martinez.

No. 500, Octagon Hotel S&C. Available in crystal, Flamingo, Sahara, Marigold, and crystal with Moongleam handles. 1928-1935. Some inventive individuals have taken the crystal sets with Moongleam handies and put them under ultraviolet lamps and turned the crystal bowls a medium shade of purple. These sets are not, "rare purple Heisey." The overall effect is striking but these pieces are essentially damaged glass. Note the handle variations from pointed to round in shape, with placements sometimes at and sometimes below the rim. Be aware of this if you want your handles to match.

Right below the creamer on the Octagon catalog page is this six inch oblong tray with no further explanation as to it's purpose. S&C collectors have long speculated that the little tray was intended to be used as an under plate for the creamer, especially since Moongleam sugars have never appeared. Side by side, it's obvious that the well of the tray isn't big enough for the base of the creamer to settle snugly into; but that hasn't stopped collectors from putting the two pieces together. The set does make a nice looking, albeit unsteady, display.
Photos above and below courtesy Jean & Vic Laermans.

No. 1170, Pleat and Panel Hotel S&C. Available in crystal, darker Moongleam, and Flamingo. Sets were sold with and without the lid. Typically found undecorated, unusual sets can be found with decorations ranging from simple to elaborate. 1925-1937.
Courtesy Ted Sheets & John Martinez.

No. 1231, Ribbed Octagon Hotel S&C. Available in crystal, Flamingo, Moongleam, and Sahara. 1929-1936.

No. 1405, Ipswitch S&C. Available in crystal, Flamingo, Moongleam, and Sahara. 1931 to mid-1930s. It's thought that crystal may have been re-released in the early 1950s for a time.
Moongleam, courtesy Kay & Dave Tucker.
Flamingo, courtesy Glynis McCain.

No. 3397, Gascony S&C. Available in crystal and Sahara. 1932-1938. Courtesy Ted Sheets & John Martinez.

No. 1401 1/2, Empress S&C with unusual round foot. Available in crystal, Flamingo, and Moongleam. Courtesy Jean & Vic Laermans.

Comparison photo between Empress round footed sugar (left) and round footed mayonnaise (right). Courtesy Dennis Headrick.

No. 1401, Empress Individual S&C on tray. S&C were sold with and without the tray. Colors available included crystal, Flamingo, Moongleam, and Sahara.

No. 1401, Empress DF (Dolphin Foot) large S&C with No. 500, Octagon tray. 1930-1938. Heisey probably never intended for the tray to go under this S&C. The Lotus Glass company put these three pieces together as a set in decorated crystal, and collectors eagerly followed their lead and put their colored sets on trays as well. Trays are found in crystal, Flamingo, Moongleam and Sahara and there aren't enough of them to go around. Courtesy Jean & Vic Laermans.

No. 1401, Empress in Alexandrite, a dichroic color which changes it's hue under different types of lighting. Above is incandescent light and florescent light is below. Other colors available were Moongleam, Tangerine, Flamingo, and Sahara. Both photos courtesy Dennis Headrick.

No, 1401, Empress (left), **No. 1509, Queen Ann** *(right).
From 1938-1957, Heisey sold a modified version of the Empress Dolphin Foot and individual sets in crystal. The new line was called No. 1509, Queen Ann. Queen Ann differs from crystal Empress in that the glass is thicker and there is a slight internal optic which enhances the external decorations. Queen Ann S&C received a variety of etchings and cuttings as well as being sold plain. Many collectors call only the colored S&C "Empress" and refer to all crystal S&C sets as Queen Ann. It is possible to tell the difference and identify the pieces properly by running one's finger around the inside of the piece and feeling for the internal optic. This is the second time Heisey used the name Queen Ann (see also No. 365, Queen Ann). Courtesy Dennis Headrick.*

No. 1469, Ridgeleigh *Hotel S&C. This cube shaped set was also known as No. 7015, Ribbed Quator at one point in time.
Courtesy Kay & Dave Tucker.*

*No. 1469, Ridgeleigh large and Individual S&C.
1935-1944. Crystal only.*

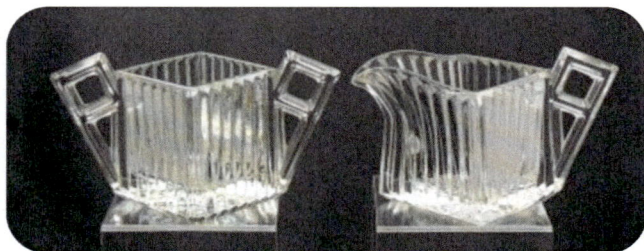

No. 1403, Half Circle *Individual S&C. Only one size was made. Available in crystal, Flamingo, Moongleam, and Sahara. Crystal is the most difficult to find. 1930-1935. Courtesy Kay & Dave Tucker.*

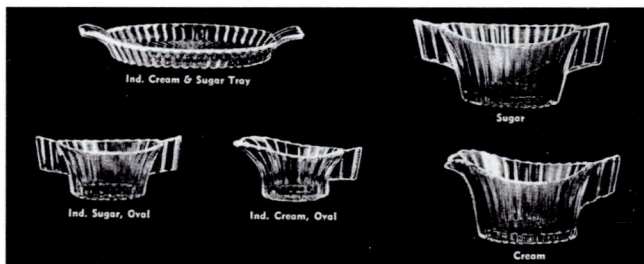

Above is the Ridgeleigh Individual sugar (left) next to a lookalike ribbed sugar (right). Notice the differences between the handles and the rim swoop. This lookalike is found in crystal, cobalt and amethyst and was made by the Hazel-Atlas company.

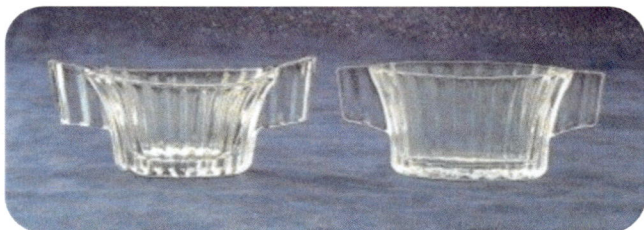

No. 1403, Half Circle colors. Courtesy Dennis Headrick.

Colors of Hazel-Atlas lookalike. Courtesy Karen Plott.

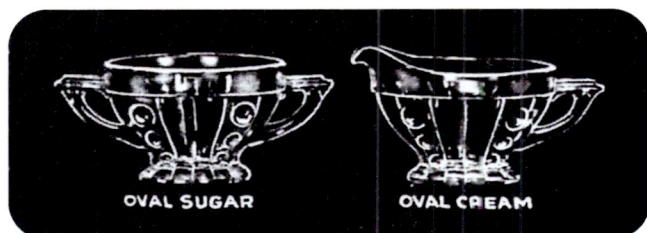

*No. 1404, **Old Sandwich** oval S&C (above and below). Available in crystal, Flamingo, Moongleam, and Sahara. 1931-1956.*

No. 1404, Old Sandwich round S&C. Crystal only. 1950s. Courtesy Kay & Dave Tucker.

*No. 1511, **Toujours** was made in both a large and Individual size. Toujours is a French word meaning "always" or "forever." Crystal only. 1939-1953. Toujours size comparison above. Both pieces have the No. 503, Minuet etching. Courtesy Kay & Dave Tucker.*

A Heisey lookalike with overall diamond pattern. Found in crystal and light blue. Trays have the word "Japan" embossed on the edge.

In the 1930s, Heisey began changing it's style of identifying all of it's sugar and creamer sets as either Table, Hotel or Individual. The large Table sets lost their popularity in the late 1920s with spooners going out of style and both sugars and creamers becoming smaller and less obtrusive. Most small S&C were still referred to as Individual, but the use of the term Hotel also began to wane. By the 1950s, many sets were simply listed in the catalogs as *sugar* or *cream*.

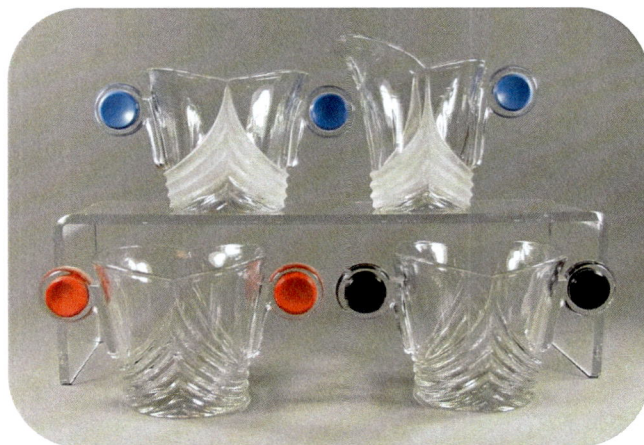

*No. 1483, **Stanhope** S&C. Crystal only. Handles are circular with plastic discs inserted through them. These discs do fall out. The S&C are typically found with black discs, but red, white and royal blue were also made. Pieces are typically found undecorated but on rare occasions, you might find the draped section satinized, the plain section with etchings or cuttings, or both decoration treatments together. 1936-1941. Courtesy Ted Sheets & John Martinez.*

No. 4044, New Era S&C. Crystal only. 1934-1941.
The set pictured above has the No. 480, Normandie etching.
The New Era blank was also manufactured with a cobalt base during
the same time period. These cobalt-based pieces are part of the
No. 2323, Navy *line and are rarely seen.*

No. 1447, Rococo S&C. Available in crystal and Sahara. 1935-1938.

No. 1495, Fern large S&C above and Individual S&C below.
Crystal only. 1937-1941.

No. 1495, Fern Individual set with unknown gold decoration.
Courtesy Kay & Dave Tucker.

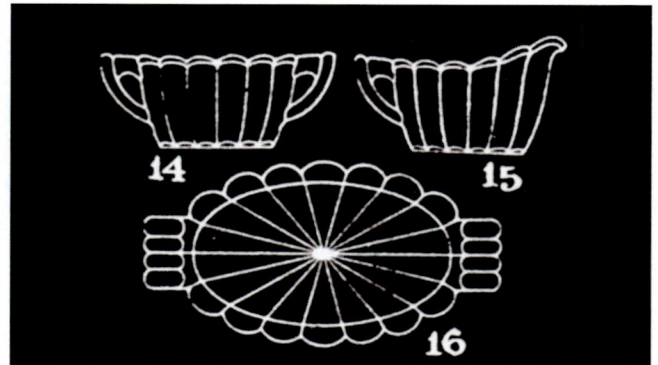

No. 1503, Crystolite Individual set showing tray detal.
Crystal only. 1938-1957. Crystolite was one of Heisey's mainstay
dinnerware lines until they closed their doors in 1957. That popularity
is reflected in the ease of obtaining both the low-set S&C sets in this
line. There is a lookalike to the Individual set which sits on it's own tray.
I've seen this lookalike in amber and crystal. In the middle of a
Crystolite sugar or creamer, the vertical panels go straight up and down.
In the middle of the lookalike, the center panels join to form a pointed
arch. It's actually a nice looking set. Buying one of these sets in error is
highly unlikely as there are 50 Crystolite sets on the secondary market
right now for every lookalike set.

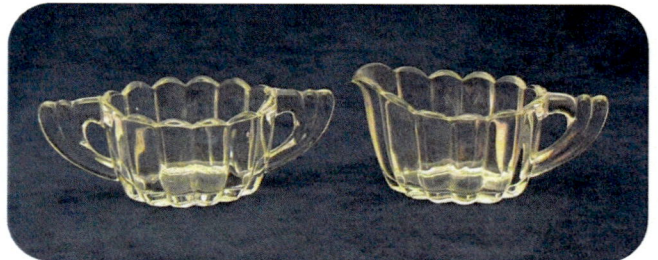

No. 1503, Crystolite large S&C. 1938-1957. Crystal only.
Silver overlays are possible.

No. 1503 1/2, Crystolite Hotel S&C. Significantly less available than
it's oval cousins shown above. Courtesy Ted Sheets & John Martinez.

No. 1425, Victorian S&C. Available in crystal and Sahara. 1933-1953. Rare Stiegel Blue (cobalt) sets are known to exist. Courtesy Karen Plott.

1950s catalog reprint.

No. 1506, Whirlpool large S&C (above) and Individual S&C with tray (below). 1938-1957. Predominantly made in crystal, the Limelight set appeared in the 1956 catalog. Limelight is the old Zircon formula with some slight differences.

After 1957, Imperial Glass remade the large set in crystal, amber, Heather (purple) and Verde green. Imperial pieces are found with Heisey logos and are frequently mislabeled as "rare" Heisey colors. This error is so common it's comedic.

*In the last years the company was in operation, they renamed the Whirlpool line: **Provincial**.*

The Individual set was only made in crystal. Individual sets which are found in red were made for the Heisey Collectors of America (HCA). Photos above and below courtesy Kay & Dave Tucker.

No. 1485, Saturn Hotel S&C. 1937-1953 (intermittently). Colors available are crystal and Zircon. The Zircon color was introduced in 1936 and only made for a few years. Courtesy Kay & Dave Tucker.

No. 1485, Saturn S&C with lid. Sugar has handles. 1947-1953. Crystal only. Courtesy Jean & Vic Laermans.

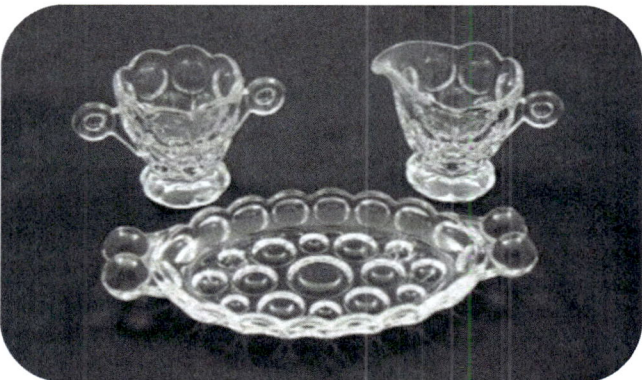

No. 1485, Saturn S&C with lid. Sugar has no handles. Crystal only. 1949-1953. Courtesy Ted Sheets & John Martinez.

*No. 1519, **Waverly** was made in both a large and Individual size. The large set has an Octagonal foot while the Individual set has a round foot. The Individual S&C sit on a tray. Waverly is known for being the canvas for two popular Heisey etchings: No. 507 Orchid and No. 515 Rose (shown here.) The tray was originally part of the No. 1401, Empress line. Trays were etched and its most desirable to display an etched S&C on a matching, etched tray. Crystal only. 1940-1957.*
All Waverly photos courtesy Kay & Dave Tucker.

*No. 7000, **Sunflower** S&C. Crystal only. 1938.*
Courtesy Ted Sheets & John Martinez.

*No. 1541, **Athena** was made by Heisey exclusively for the Montgomery Ward catalog in the mid to late 1940s. Crystal only. After the Ward campaign was finished, Heisey continued making the sugar and creamer for a short time.*
The same S-shaped scroll design element which surrounds the rim of the tray is repeated on the sugar and creamer in a "necklace" which goes around the stem of the sugar and creamer.
Pieces decorated with cuttings, like those shown here, were from the later Heisey period and are rare.
Photo courtesy Ted Sheets & John Martinez.

*No. 1533, **Wampum** S&C. Crystal only. 1941-1942.*
Similar to Sunflower with the addition of a beaded accent.

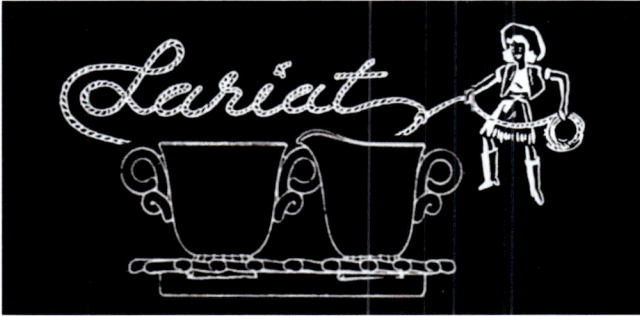

No. 1540, Lariat was made in one size only. S&C sets were sold with or without a tray. Crystal only. 1942-1957. 1950s catalog illustration.

Many different decorations can be found on the Lariat blanks. One could make it a collecting passion trying to find all the different cuttings, etchings, overlays, and hand paintings. Decorations were done both by Heisey and outside decorating companies. Unknown decoration shown. Courtesy Dennis Headrick.

Lariat with Charleton Rose by Abels, Wasserberg, & Co. Courtesy Red Toler.

No. 1590, Zodiac S&C. The S&C contain panels illustrating the (then) twelve accepted signs of the zodiac. The sugar and creamer each contain six different panels. 1940-1950. Crystal only. Imperial Glass reissued the set in crystal, amber and Verde green. Courtesy Ted Sheets & John Martinez.

No. 1567, Plantation S&C. Sold with or without a "pineapple" tray. Crystal only. 1948-1957. It is not unusual to find this set with the No. 516, Plantation Ivy etching. The decoration shown above is a unique sand-etching from an outside decorating company. Photo above courtesy Ted Sheets & John Martinez.

No. 1567, Plantation tray. Courtesy Kay & Dave Tucker.

No. 341, Old Williamsburg S&C. Courtesy Ted Sheets & John Martinez.

*Known as **Nos. 1626, Satellite** in crystal and **1632, Lodestar** in Dawn. This S&C were made in the mid-1950s. All crystal creamers are handle-less as are most Dawn creamers. The Dawn variant with the handle is the more difficult creamer to find. Crystal pieces are even more elusive and they were probably produced for only one year while Dawn was produced for two or more.*
Photos (above and below) courtesy Dennis Headrick.

Dawn was introduced in 1955 and it was the last new color which Heisey produced. Heisey closed it's doors at the end of 1957.

The **No. 341, Old Williamsburg** line consisted of popular pieces from several colonial-styled lines. S&C sets which were at one time or another included in the Old Williamsburg line were: No. 300, Hotel and Individual sets, No. 351 Hotel set, and No. 352 Hotel set. Crystal only. 1939-1957. For clarification, these sets are all refered to and priced under their original line numbers. The set shown at left first appeared as part of the Old Williamsburg line in the 1950 catalog. After Imperial Glass acquired the Heisey molds, they reissued this set alongside the No. 300 Hotel and Individual sets continuing with the name "Old Williamsburg."

No. 1951, Cabochon in Dawn. Courtesy Ted Sheets & John Martinez.

The **No. 1951, Cabochon** S&C were made in crystal from 1951-1957. The color Dawn was only made during 1955. The crystal set was sold with or without the lid and with or without the tray. Imperial Glass also made the lid and tray. Even though the lid and tray were made by both companies, neither of those pieces are easy to find. The tray is particularly elusive. Neither the lid nor the tray were known to have been made in Dawn. After a time, Imperial changed the name of this set to "Revere" and removed the tray and lid from it's inventory. Sets with rock-crystal type cuttings were done by both Heisey and Imperial.

Imperial catalog reprint.

Pricing	Crystal Sugar with lid	Crystal Creamer or lidless sugar	Decorated or colors
#341, Old Williamsburg Hotel (1950-1957)		$10	+ 20% for metal base
#355, Quator Hotel flat		$7 +	
#355, Quator Individual		$19 +	
#355, Quator Hotel footed		trtp	Flamingo and Moongleam $20
#360, Corby Hotel	trtp	trtp	
#411, Tudor footed	$34 +	$18 +	
#411, Tudor Hotel	$20 (crystal lid)	$9 +	Crystal with Mnglm handles sugar or creamer $24 Hawthorne creamer $38, Hawthorn sugar w/lid $70
#412, Tudor sugar no handles		trtp	
#414, Tudor sugar no handles		trtp	all colors trtp
#452, Hotel		trtp	
#479, Petal Hotel		trtp	Flamingo $22, Moongleam $26, Flamingo $38, Hawthorne $65 *SAHARA??*
#485, Dunham Table	trtp	trtp	
#500, Octagon Hotel		trtp	Crystal w/ Mnglm $12, Sahara, Flamingo $17, Moongleam $35
#500, Octagon tray			all colors trtp
#1001, Casewell	$25 + (Mnglm foot)	$25 + (Mnglm foot)	Flamingo pieces $34, Hawthorne trtp, add 20% for glass lids
#1020, Phyllis Hotel		$12 +	Flamingo $18, dark Moongleam $32, Moongleam $37, Canary trtp
#1021, Christine Hotel	$14 +	$8 +	
#1022, Harding Hotel	trtp	trtp	
#1023, Hotel	$25 +	$20 +	
#1024, Eileen Hotel	$10 +	$6 +	
#1025, Sharon Hotel	$12 +	$8 +	
#1170, Pleat and Panel Hotel	$15 +	$12 +	Flamingo sugar w/ lid $25, Moongleam sugar w/ lid $42
#1180, Debra Hotel	$14 +	$6 +	
#1181, Revere Individual		$10 +	
#1182, Revere Individual		$10 + (creamer)	sugar trtp
#1183, Revere footed		$10 +	
#1183, Revere Individual		$8 +	
#1183, Revere Hotel oval		$6 +	
#1183, Revere footed tall	trtp	trtp	
#1183 1/2, Revere Individual		$16 +	
#1184, Yeoman Hotel	$8 +	$7 +	Flamingo, Sahara sugars $22, Moongleam sugar $25, Hawthorne sugar $45, add 30% to pieces without diamond optic Pieces with etchings start at 2x plain value
#1184, Yeoman stack set	$14 +	$8 +	
#1184, Yeoman Individual cream		trtp	all colors trtp
#1185, Yeoman Hotel round		$8 +	
#1185, Yeoman Individual round		$14 +	
#1186, Yeoman Hotel oval		$8 +	
#1189, Yeoman footed	trtp	trtp	
#1190, Yeoman Hotel oval		trtp	
#1231, Ribbed Octagon Hotel		$5 +	Flamingo, Sahara $8, Moongleam $12
#1252, Twist Hotel flat		trtp	all colors trtp
#1252, Twist Hotel ftd		trtp	Flamingo $85+, Moongleam $105+
#1252, Twist Hotel oval		trtp	Flamingo, Sahara $40, Moongleam $45, Marigold $67
#1252, Twist Individual		trtp	Flamingo $32, Moongleam $40, Marigold trtp
#1401, Empress DF		$9 +	Sahara $16 +, Flamingo $19, Moongleam $24, Alexandrite $150 Tangerine trtp
#1401, Empress Individual		$7	Flamingo, Sahara $14, Moongleam $22
#1401, Empress Individual tray		$15	Flamingo $30, Sahara and Moongleam trtp
#1401 1/2, Empress round foot		trtp	all colors trtp
#1403, Half Circle Individual		$18	Sahara $23, Flamingo $28, Moongleam $30

Pricing	Crystal Sugar with lid	Crystal Creamer or lidless sugar	Decorated or colors
#1404, Old Sandwich oval		$12	Sahara $38
#1404, Old Sandwich round		trtp	
#1405, Ipswich		$13	all colors trtp
#1425, Victorian		$8	all colors trtp
#1447, Rococo		trtp	Sahara trtp
#1469, Ridgeleigh Hotel		$30	
#1469, Ridgeleigh large		<$5	
#1469, Ridgeleigh Individual		$5	tray $10
#1483, Stanhope		black handle $20, all other colors trtp +	
#1485, Saturn Hotel		$22	Zircon trtp
#1485, Saturn w/handles	$18	$11	
#1485, Saturn w/o handles	$25	$11	
#1495, Fern large		$17 +	
#1495, Fern Individual		$36 +	
#1503, Crystolite large		<$5	2x for silver overlay
#1503, Crystolite Individual		$5	tray $10
#1503 1/2, Crystolite Hotel		$16	
#1506, Whirlpool large		$5	Zircon $65
#1506, Whirlpool Individual		$6	tray $12
#1509, Queen Ann DF		$8 +	
#1509, Queen Ann Individual		$8 +	tray $15 +
#1511, Toujours large		$9 +	
#1511, Toujours Individual		$19 +	
#1519, Waverly large		<$5 +	Orchid etch $7, Rose etch $14
#1519, Waverly Individual		$5 +	Orchid etch $9, Rose etch $20
#1519, Waverly Individual tray		$10	Orchid etch $36, Rose etch $44
#1533, Wampum		$12	
#1540, Lariat		<$5 +	Charleton Rose decoration $32, tray $9
#1541, Athena		$15 +	tray $22
#1567, Plantation		$11 +	Ivy decoration $17, tray $55
#1590, Zodiac		$7	
#1626, Satellite		trtp	
#1632, Lodestar		$39 (no handles)	$55 creamer w/ handles
#1951, Cabochon	$19	$6 +	Dawn $30, tray $16
#2323, Navy		trtp	
#3397, Gascony		trtp	Sahara trtp
#4044, New Era		$9 +	
#4222, Horseshoe		trtp	Sahara $100, all other colors trtp
#7000, Sunflower		$8	
#7068, Four Arch		trtp	
#8061, Lodi		trtp	

+ Decorated pieces price higher and it would be impossible to list even a portion of the decorations available in this space. Simple cuttings add 20%, simple silver overlays add 30%. Prices escalate from there based on condition of the decoration, complexity, and desirability. Decorations with a known identity generally price higher than unknown decorations. Decorations from collectible companies such as Lotus Glass, Farber Brothers, Rockwell Silver, or the Wheeling Decorating Company will price higher than less collectible decorations. Some Heisey decorations were mass produced, others are scarce or rare. Some decorations like the Charleton Rose are not rare, but they are beloved and that keeps their price at a premium. Cornflower cuttings are quite popular in Canada because the artisans who created them lived in Canada; but in the United States the market for Cornflower cuttings isn't as active. Take your time and buy what you love.

ANCHOR HOCKING

Cameo - Average prices for Domino trays have dropped to the $150 range, with one recent tray selling for as low as $110. Internet supply seems to have increased and this should balance itself out as the available trays find their way into private collections.

Mayfair - A yellow sugar and lid surfaced at auction and the pair sold for $1548. This surprised me in that not only is the lid rare, but so is the sugar bowl. The pair should have priced higher than the $2000 average for pink lids indicating a strong color preference for pink amongst collectors. Photo courtesy Frank Forsythe.

Charm - A company catalog has surfaced showing the forest green Charm being sold on an oval crystal tray. The S&C only fit on the tray one way due to the handles and the set doesn't look like it belongs together. Trays are 8 3/16" long.

Swirl - An unusual Peacock decoration has appeared on the gold trimmed white set.

BARTLETT-COLLINS

Sheraton - The stacking set has appeared in crystal, finally.

Ellipse - A pink enamel S&C has appeared to go along with the light blue set already known.

No. 87 - A new etching has been found (see above). No known name or number.

No. 1500 - Satinized and hand-painted pieces have surfaced with original labels from the *Rita Novelty Company*. These painted sets come with several different colored flowers

CAMBRIDGE

Martha Washington - The No. 14 squat S&C set has appeared in Heatherbloom.

Decagon - The No. 1076 set has appeared in dark green on the No. 1095 crystal lightning handle tray. Other colors which have also made an appearance in No. 1076 are light green and pink.

The No. 1095 tray has appeared in green with a satinized handle but no S&C was with it so it is unknown which set was intended to be sold with this unusual tray.

Nos. 134 & 2800/4 - They are easy to confuse. No 134 is shown in Azurite and No. 2800/4 is shown in black. No. 134 has a round foot and No. 2800/4 has an octagonal foot. By far and away, No. 134 is the easiest to find.

No. 620 - After stating that the 2-place trays never seem to appear in crystal, I've seen two.

No. 3400/98 - **Error Correction p. 69.** The pricing shown for the ball shaped S&C does not include the metal Farber Brothers holder. Add $20 to the prices shown for sets sold in holders. Add $15 to the prices shown for single pieces sold with the holder. Holders by themselves sell for $20.

Caprice - The No. 40, individual S&C set has appeared in pink. S&C continue to occasionally appear in a lavender color and I've been unable to examine any pieces; but I wonder if they aren't crystal pieces being turned with an ultraviolet light.

CANTON

Peerless - Canton's Heisey lookalike has been found in cobalt. This is not Imperial. Refer to page 108 of this book.

CENTRAL

No. 1450 tray - Amber is the only color I've seen other than black and this is the only amber tray I've ever seen. The tray has distinctive ribbing on the underside which isn't seen in the photos of the black trays. Look for this design element. Photo courtesy Dave Lippert.

DIAMOND

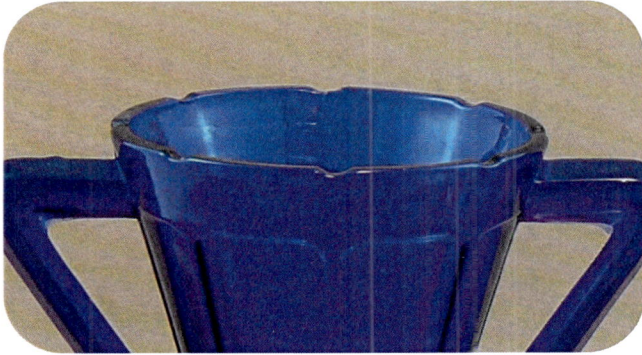

Victory - The black S&C shown in Book 1 doesn't show the notches in the rim clearly. Here is a close-up photo.

DUNCAN

Hobnail - The S&C have been found on the scallop edged tray shown. This tray is shown in the Hobnail advertisement reprinted in Book 1.

Canterbury - The Individual size has appeared in plain blue (no opalescence). This gives me hope that a plain pink Individual set might appear at some time.

Radiance - I suspected that the Radiance S&C had been made in cobalt and now there is proof. Radiance has appeared in cobalt (and green too).

No. 50 - I wanted to share this silver overlay which has been found on No. 50. I have no information about the decorating company but I think it's fabulous. Photo courtesy Karen Plott.

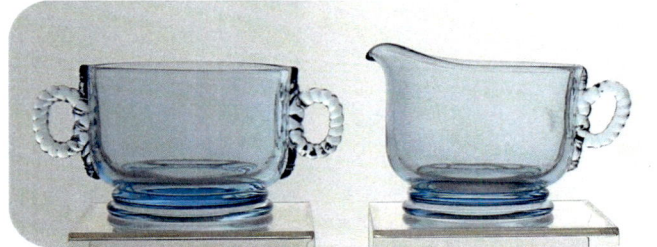

Nautical - In Book 1, I showed a sales brochure reprint which illustrated the S&C with a rope motif on the base. Apparently, the designers vision never reached production because the actual set has a plain base. The 1935 catalog confirms this plain base.

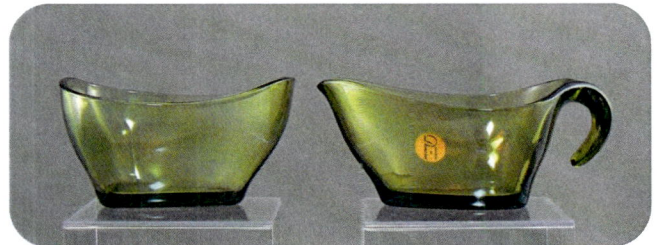

Laguna - Full sets are being uncovered which allow us to see the actual profile of the sugar bowl. A Teakwood Brown set sold for $85 in 2014. Photo courtesy Dick Ladd.

Terrace - More wonderful decorations are showing up on this delightful set including a crystal satin with cut-to-clear floral embellishments. Lotus Glass used this set for some of their etchings. One collector has noticed that sets done by Duncan will have etchings on the lid; but Lotus did not seem to put etchings on the lid. The etching shown here is an unknown.

There are two new additions to the Duncan family. No line numbers have been identified for the sets below so I gave them names for identification purposes.

Alta - Notice the characteristic curl at the top of the handle ala Canterbury. These pieces appear with Duncan's sand etchings. The set shown is sand etched with the *Magnolia* design.

Brighton - Found with the *First Love* etching. Once again, this set exhibits the classic Duncan

handle swoop. The creamer is similar in shape to the Alta creamer shown, but with the ruffled rim.

FEDERAL

Rope - Crystal Rope found with floral decals.

Madrid - **Error Correction p. 137.** In the second photo showing the blue Recollection next to the blue Madrid, the pieces are identified incorrectly. Recollection is on the left and Madrid is on the right.

Sharon - Sharon continues to be reproduced in new colors. Now there is a green reproduction to watch for. Amber remains the only Federal color which hasn't been reproduced.

Greenbrier and Dura-white - New decorations.

All photos this column courtesy Karen Plott.

INDEX

15282164R00085

Made in the USA
Middletown, DE
30 October 2014